The Tankadère signals for help. (*Page* 114)

AROUND THE WORLD
IN EIGHTY DAYS

By
JULES VERNE

WARD, LOCK & CO., LIMITED
LONDON AND MELBOURNE

MADE IN ENGLAND
Printed in Great Britain by Butler & Tanner Ltd., Frome and London

CONTENTS

CONTENTS

CHAPTER I

*In which Phileas Fogg and Passepartout accept the
positions of master and servant respectively*

In the year 1872 the house, No. 7, Savile Row, Bur-
lington Gardens, in which Sheridan died in 1816, was
occupied by Phileas Fogg, Esquire, one of the most
remarkable members of the Reform Club, though he
always appeared very anxious to avoid remark.

Phileas Fogg had succeeded to the house of one of
the greatest of English orators; but, unlike his predecessor, no one knew anything of Fogg; he was an
enigmatical personage, though brave, and moving in
the highest circles. It was said that he resembled
Byron, merely in features, for his morals were irre-
proachable, but he was a Byron with moustaches and
whiskers—an impassive Byron, one who might get to
a thousand years without getting old.

Though perhaps not a Londoner, Phileas Fogg was
English to the backbone. He was never seen on the
Stock Exchange, nor at the Bank, nor in any City
house. No vessel consigned to Phileas Fogg ever
entered the London Docks; he held no position under
Government; he was not a lawyer at any of the Inns;
he had never pleaded at the Queen's Bench, the Chan-
cery Bar, the Exchequer, nor the Ecclesiastical Courts;
he was not a manufacturer, nor a merchant, nor a
farmer; he was not a member of any of the learned
societies of the metropolis. He was simply a member
of the Reform Club.

If anyone asked how he had become a member of
such a distinguished club, he was told that he had
been proposed by the Barings, who kept his account,
which always showed a good balance, and his cheques
were regularly honoured.

Was Phileas Fogg rich? Not a doubt of it. But

not even the best informed could say how he had made his money, and Fogg was the last person in the world from whom the information could be obtained. He was never extravagant, but not stingy, for whenever his assistance was required for some useful or praiseworthy object he gave willingly and anonymously.

In short, he was one of the most taciturn of men; he spoke as seldom as possible, and appeared more mysterious in consequence of his silence. Nevertheless his life was sufficiently open, but it was so mathematically arranged that to the imagination of the curious this circumstance rendered it more suspicious.

Had he travelled? Very likely, for no one knew more about geography than he did. There was no corner of the earth but he had some exclusive information respecting it. Sometimes in a few brief sentences he would clear up the rumours in his club respecting some lost or almost forgotten travellers; he would indicate the probabilities, and it would almost seem as if he possessed the gift of second-sight, so correctly were his anticipations subsequently justified. He must have been everywhere, in spirit at least.

However, one thing was quite certain. He had not been away from London for years. His most intimate acquaintance could declare that he had never been seen anywhere else but at his club, or on his way to and from it. His only amusement was a game of whist or reading the newspapers. At whist, which suited his taciturn disposition, he was generally a winner, but he always spent his winnings in charity. Besides, it is worth notice that he always played for the game, not for the sake of making money. He played as a trial of skill, a fight against difficulties, but a contest in which no exertion was entailed upon him; he had not to move about nor to fatigue himself, and this suited him thoroughly.

No one knew whether Fogg had a wife or children, which might be possessed by the most scrupulously honest of men; nor whether he had relations or intimate friends, which are rare enough in all conscience. He lived alone in Savile Row, and no one ever called. He only kept one servant, he breakfasted and dined at his club at regular hours, at the same table, but he never asked an acquaintance to join him, nor did he ever invite a stranger; he went home to bed at midnight exactly, and he never occupied one of the comfortable bedrooms at the Reform. Of the twenty-four hours he spent ten at his own house, either asleep or at his toilette. If he took exercise it was in the hall at the club, with its mosaic pavement, or in the circular gallery, supported by twenty Ionic columns. Here he would walk up and down. When he dined or breakfasted, all the cooks, the steward, and the resources of the club were exercised to supply his table. He was waited upon by grave servants dressed in black, who walked softly as they served him upon a special porcelain set, and with the most expensive damask. His sherry was handed to him in priceless decanters and iced to a nicety, and the port and claret were of the finest vintages.

If life under such conditions be any proof of eccentricity, it must be confessed that eccentricity has its good side.

The house in Savile Row, though not luxurious, was very comfortable; besides, in accordance with the habits of the owner, the service was reduced as much as possible, but Phileas Fogg was most particular as regards punctuality. On the very day we are introduced to him (the 2nd of October), he had given his servant, James Foster, notice because he had had the temerity to bring up his master's shaving-water at a temperature of 84 degrees instead of 86 degrees, and

7

Phileas was now waiting a successor, who was expected between eleven and half-past eleven o'clock.

Phileas Fogg was seated in his armchair, his feet at "attention," his hands resting on his knees, his body upright, and his head erect. He was watching the clock. This complex piece of machinery told the hours, minutes, seconds, the days of the week, month, and year. When the chime of half-past eleven rang out, Mr. Fogg would leave the house for his club.

Just then a knock was heard at the door of the little sitting-room, and James Foster appeared.

"The new valet has come, sir," he said.

A young fellow of about thirty entered, and bowed to Mr. Fogg.

"You are a Frenchman, and your name is John?" said Mr. Fogg.

"Jean, if it is all the same to you, sir," replied the newcomer. "Jean Passepartout—a name which will stick to me, and which will be justified by my natural aptitude for change. I believe I am honest; but, to tell the truth, I have tried a great many things. I have been an itinerant singer, a circus-rider, an acrobat like Leotard, and a rope-walker like Blondin, then I became a professor of gymnastics, and at last, to make myself useful, I enrolled myself as a fireman in Paris, and can show you the scars of several burns. But it is now five years since I left France, and as I wished to enjoy domestic life I became a valet in England. Now being without a situation, and having heard that Mr. Phileas Fogg was the most punctual and the most sedentary gentleman in the United Kingdom, I have taken the liberty to come here for a quiet life, and to forget my name of Passepartout."

"Passepartout suits me," replied Mr. Fogg. "You have been recommended to me. You know my conditions?"

" Yes, sir."

" Well, what time do you make it?"

" Twenty-two minutes past eleven," replied Passepartout, pulling out an enormous silver watch.

" You are slow," said Mr. Fogg.

" Excuse me, sir, that is impossible."

" You are four minutes behind time. Never mind ;
it is sufficient to have made a note of it. Well then,
from this moment, twenty-nine minutes past eleven
a.m., the 2nd of October, 1872, you are in my service."

As he spoke, Mr. Fogg rose, took up his hat in his
left hand, put it on his head automatically, and left
the room without another word.

Passepartout heard the door shut once—that was his
master going out; he heard it shut a second time—
that was his predecessor, James Foster, who was leaving in his turn.

Passepartout was left alone in the house in Savile Row.

CHAPTER II

Passepartout is convinced he has found his ideal

" Egad," said Passepartout, who was rather flurried for
the minute, " I have seen figures at Madame Tussaud's
quite as cheerful as my new master."

It may be remarked that Madame Tussaud's figures
are of wax, and want nothing but the power of speech.

During the short time that Passepartout had been
in the society of Mr. Fogg he had scrutinized him
carefully. His future master seemed to be about forty,
tall and well made, not too stout, and with noble,
handsome features. His hair and whiskers were fair,
his brow was open, his face rather pale, and he had
beautiful teeth. He appeared to possess in a high
degree that which physiognomists call repose in action
—a faculty common to all those who prefer deeds to

9

words. Calm, phlegmatic, with clear steady eyes, he was a type of those cool Englishmen whom one frequently meets, and who have been so well portrayed by Angelica Kauffmann. In his everyday life Mr. Fogg gave one the idea of a perfectly-balanced being —a sort of chronometer—in fact, he was punctuality personified, and so much could be seen in the " expression of his hands and feet," for with men, as amongst the lower animals, the members are expressive of passions. Phileas Fogg was one of those people who are never in a hurry, and being always ready are economical of their movements. He never took a step too much; he always went the shortest way. He never wasted a look at the ceiling, and never permitted himself a needless gesture. No one had ever seen him agitated or annoyed; he never hurried himself, but was always in time. He lived alone, and, so to speak, outside the social scale; he knew that there was a great deal of friction in life, and as friction retards progress he never rubbed against anyone.

As for Passepartout, he was a Parisian of Parisians. For five years he had lived in England as *valet-de-chambre*, during which time he had vainly sought for such a master as he had now engaged himself to.

Passepartout was not one of those Frontins or Mascarilles who with high shoulders and snub noses are only dunces; he was a good fellow, with pleasant features, ruddy lips ready to kiss or to eat, a good-natured serviceable lad, possessing one of those round heads which one is so glad to see on the shoulders of one's friends. He had blue eyes; his face was somewhat stout; he was very strong and muscular. He wore his brown hair in rather a ragged fashion. If sculptors of antiquity knew eighteen ways of arranging the hair of Minerva, Passepartout knew only one way of arranging his—three strokes of a comb was sufficient for him.

To say that the young man's character would agree with Mr. Fogg's would be rash; whether Passepartout would suit his master remained to be proved—time will tell. After having passed his youth in such a vagabond fashion the lad looked forward to some repose. He had often heard of the English methodical way of living, but up to the present time he had not succeeded in finding it. He had "taken root" nowhere, and he had tried six situations—in each there was something which did not suit him. His latest proprietor, young Lord Longsferry, M.P., had passed his nights in questionable society, and had ended by being carried home by policemen. Passepartout, who wished above all things to respect his master, remonstrated. His suggestion was taken in ill part, and he discharged himself. Just then he heard that Phileas Fogg was in want of a valet, and offered himself for the situation. A person whose existence was so methodical, who never slept away from home, who never travelled, who was never away for a day, was the very master for him. He presented himself and was successful, as we already know.

So Passepartout, at half-past eleven o'clock, found himself alone in the house. He immediately commenced to look about him, and explored the house from cellar to garret. He was very much pleased; the house seemed like a very pretty snail-shell, but a shell warmed and lighted. Passepartout soon found his room on the second floor, and was quite satisfied with it. Electric bells and acoustic tubes put him in communication with the rooms below. On the chimney-piece was an electric clock corresponding exactly with that in Mr. Fogg's bedroom—the pendulums beat time to a second.

"This will do," said Passepartout to himself.

He observed also in his room that a notice was fixed

11

above the clock; this was a programme of his daily service from eight in the morning, when Mr. Fogg got up, till half-past eleven, when he went down to his club. It included all details: the tea and toast at twenty-three minutes past eight, the shaving-water at thirty-seven minutes past nine, his attendance on his master at twenty minutes to ten, etc. Then from half-past eleven a.m. till midnight, when this methodical gentleman went to bed, everything was provided for. Passepartout was delighted, and joyfully sat down to master the details of the programme.

His master's wardrobe was well stocked and marvellously neat. Every article bore a number and was noted in a book which showed at what seasons certain suits were to be worn. The same regulations were applied to boots and shoes.

In fact, in this house in Savile Row, which had been the temple of disorder in the days of Sheridan, order now reigned supreme. There was no library and there were no books; but these would have been useless to Mr. Fogg, as there was a capital library and a reading-room at his club. In his bedroom was a safe both burglar-proof and fireproof. There were no fire-arms in the house, nor any weapons of war or for sport. Everything denoted that the occupant was a man of most pacific character.

After having examined everything in detail, Passepartout rubbed his hands; his round face beamed with joy as he said:

" This will do for me very nicely. We understand each other thoroughly, Mr. Fogg and I. He is a most domestic individual—a perfect machine. Well, I am not sorry to serve a machine after all."

CHAPTER III

A conversation which is likely to prove expensive to Phileas Fogg

Phileas Fogg left his house at half-past eleven, and having placed his right foot before his left five hundred and seventy-five times, and his left foot before his right five hundred and seventy-six times, he reached the Reform Club. He immediately went to the breakfast-room and took his place at the usual table near one of the open windows. His breakfast consisted of one *hors d'œuvre*, a piece of boiled fish, a slice of underdone beef with mushrooms, rhubarb and gooseberry tart, and some Cheshire cheese, the whole washed down with some excellent tea, which is a speciality of the Reform Club.

At forty-seven minutes past twelve he went into the sitting-room, a magnificent apartment hung with splendid pictures. A servant handed him an uncut copy of *The Times*, which Fogg himself cut and folded with the dexterity begotten of long practice. The perusal of this paper occupied him until forty-five minutes past three, and the *Standard*, which succeeded, lasted till dinner, which was eaten under similar conditions to his breakfast.

At twenty minutes to six he returned to the drawing-room and read the *Morning Chronicle*.

Half-an-hour later several members of the club came in and stood with their backs to the fire. These were Mr. Fogg's usual partners at whist, and were all enthusiastic players. They were Andrew Stuart, the engineer, John Sullivan and Samuel Fallentin, bankers, Thomas Flanagan, a brewer, and Gauthier Ralph, one of the directors of the Bank of England, all men of wealth and standing, even in that club which includes so many members of consequence in financial and business circles.

" Well, Ralph," said Flanagan, " how about this robbery?"

" Oh," said Stuart, " the Bank will lose the money."

" I expect not," said Ralph. " I fancy we shall be able to catch the thief. There are very clever detectives at all the principal ports in Europe and America, and the fellow will find it difficult to escape."

" They have the description of the thief, I suppose?" said Stuart.

" In the first place he is not a thief at all," replied Ralph seriously.

" What! do you not call a man a robber who has made away with fifty-five thousand pounds in banknotes?"

" No," replied Gauthier Ralph.

" He is a man of business, then," said John Sullivan.

" The *Morning Chronicle* says he is a gentleman."

This observation was made by Phileas Fogg, who rose up from the sea of paper surrounding him, and greeted his friends.

The subject of discussion, which all the papers of the kingdom had taken up, was a certain robbery which had been committed three days before—namely, on the 29th of September. A pile of bank-notes to the amount of fifty-five thousand pounds had been abstracted from the counter at the Bank of England.

What astonished everybody was the fact that the theft had been so easily managed, and Gauthier Ralph took the trouble to explain that when the fifty-five thousand pounds were stolen, the cashier was industriously entering a sum of three shillings and sixpence, and of course could not have his eyes everywhere.

It may be remarked in passing, and this may account for the robbery, that the Bank of England has great faith in the honesty of the public. There are no guards nor commissionaires, or gratings; gold, silver, and notes are freely exposed, and, so to speak, at the mercy of the first comer. No one is suspected. One of the closest observers of British customs has related the following experience:

One day he was in the Bank parlour, and had the curiosity to examine an ingot of gold weighing six or seven pounds which happened to be on the table. He took up the nugget, and when he had satisfied his curiosity he passed it to his neighbour. He in turn passed it to the next man, and so on; the nugget went from hand to hand to the end of a long corridor, and was not returned to its place for half-an-hour, and all the time the cashier never looked up.

But on the 29th of September matters did not go so smoothly. The package of bank-notes was not returned, and when the clock in the "drawing office" struck five, at which hour the Bank is closed, fifty-five thousand pounds was written off to profit and loss.

As soon as the robbery was ascertained to be a fact, the most able detectives were sent down to Liverpool, Glasgow, Havre, to Suez, to Brindisi, and New York, etc., with a promise of a reward (if successful) of two thousand pounds, and five per cent. on the amount recovered. In the meantime these detectives were directed to take particular notice of all travellers arriving at or departing from these ports.

Now, as the *Morning Chronicle* said, there was some reason to think that the thief was not a member of a gang at all. More than once on the 29th of September a gentlemanly, well-dressed man had been frequently remarked in the Bank near the place where the robbery had been committed. An exact description of this gentleman had been furnished to all the detectives, and so some hopeful persons, amongst whom was Gauthier Ralph, believed that the thief could not possibly escape.

Of course the robbery was the chief topic of conversation everywhere. The probabilities of success were discussed, and it is not surprising that the members of the Reform Club were also interested, particularly as one of the deputy governors of the Bank belonged to the club.

Mr. Ralph had no doubt of the ultimate success of the search because of the reward offered, which would stimulate the brains of the detectives, but his friend Andrew Stuart was of a different opinion. The discussion between these gentlemen was continued even at the whist-table, where Stuart was Flanagan's partner, and Fallentin played with Phileas Fogg. They did not argue while they played, but between the rubbers conversation waxed warm.

" I maintain that the odds are in favour of the thief," said Stuart. " He must be a sharp fellow."

" But," replied Ralph, " where can he go to?"

" What do you say?"

" Where can he go to?"

" I don't know," replied Stuart, " but there are plenty of places in the world for him."

" There used to be," said Phileas Fogg in an undertone. " Will you cut, please?" he added, passing the cards to Flanagan.

The conversation ceased for the moment, but Andrew Stuart took it up again by saying:

" Used to be! What do you mean by that? Has the world grown smaller by any chance?"

" Of course it has," replied Ralph. " I agree with Mr. Fogg the world has grown smaller, because you can go round it ten times more quickly than you could a hundred years ago; so the search for a thief will be more rapid."

" And render the escape of the thief easier also."

" Your lead, Mr. Stuart," said Phileas Fogg.

16

But the incredulous Stuart would not be convinced, and when the " hand " was finished he continued.

" It must be confessed, Mr. Ralph," he said, " that you have discovered that in one sense the world has grown smaller, because you can go round it in three months."

" In eighty days," said Phileas Fogg.

" That is right, gentlemen," added John Sullivan, " for, since the opening of the Great Indian Peninsular Railway between Rothal and Allahabad it can be done in that time. Here is the estimate given by the *Morning Chronicle*:

From London to Suez by Mont Cenis and Brindisi. Rail and Steamer . . .	7 days
From Suez to Bombay. Steamer . .	13 days
From Bombay to Calcutta. Railway .	3 days
From Calcutta to Hong Kong. Steamer .	13 days
From Hong Kong to Yokohama. Steamer	6 days
From Yokohama to San Francisco. Steamer	22 days
From San Francisco to New York. Railway	7 days
From New York to London. Steamer and Railway	9 days
Total . . .	80 days

" Yes, eighty days," cried Stuart, who unfortunately made a misdeal; " but that does not take into consideration bad weather, contrary winds, shipwreck, or railway accident."

" All included," replied Fogg as he continued to play, for this time the discussion did not cease with the deal.

" But suppose Hindoos or Indians take up the rail,

stop the trains, pillage the baggage, and scalp the travellers?"

"All included," returned Fogg quietly. "Two by honours," he added.

Stuart, who was "pony," took up the cards and said:

"In theory, no doubt, you are right, Mr. Fogg, but in practice——"

"In practice too, Mr. Stuart."

"I should like to see you do it."

"It rests with you. Suppose we go together?"

"Heaven forbid!" exclaimed Stuart, "but I will bet you four thousand pounds that the thing is impossible in the time."

"On the contrary, it is quite possible," replied Mr. Fogg.

"Well, then, do it."

"Go round the world in eighty days?"

"Yes."

"I will."

"When?"

"At once."

"Ah! that is all nonsense," exclaimed Stuart, who was beginning to be vexed at his partner's insistence. "Let us continue the game."

"You must deal, then," replied Fogg; "the last is a misdeal."

Andrew Stuart took up the cards in an uncertain manner, and put them down again.

"Well, then, Mr. Fogg," he said, "I will bet you four thousand pounds——"

"My dear Stuart," said Fallentin, "don't be absurd. He is not serious."

"When I say I bet," replied Andrew Stuart, "I am quite serious."

"All right," said Mr. Fogg; then, turning to his friends, he said:

"I have twenty thousand pounds deposited with Baring Brothers. I will willingly risk that sum."

"Twenty thousand pounds!" exclaimed John Sullivan. "You might lose it all by some unforeseen accident."

"The unforeseen does not exist," replied Phileas Fogg simply.

"But, Mr. Fogg, this eighty days is but the minimum of time."

"A minimum well employed is sufficient."

"But in order not to exceed it you must pass with mathematical certainty from railways to steamers, and from steamers to railways."

"I will be accurate."

"After all, this can be but a joke."

"A true Briton never jokes when he has a bet depending on a subject. I bet you twenty thousand pounds that I will go round the world in eighty days or less—that is to say, in nineteen hundred and twenty hours, or a hundred and fifteen thousand two hundred minutes. Will you take it?"

"Yes," replied the others after consultation.

"Very well, then," replied Mr. Fogg; "the Continental Mail starts at eight-forty-five, and we will go by it."

"This evening!" exclaimed Stuart.

"This evening," replied Fogg. Then, looking at a pocket almanac, he continued: "This is Wednesday the 2nd of October; I shall be in London in this room on Saturday evening the 21st of December, at a quarter before nine p.m.; if not the twenty thousand pounds at Barings' will be yours. Here is my cheque for that sum."

A memorandum to this effect was written out and signed on the spot. Phileas Fogg was perfectly cool. He had certainly not bet to win the money, and he had only staked twenty thousand pounds, half of his fortune, because he knew he might have to spend the other moiety in carrying out his almost impossible project. His adversaries were quite excited, not because of the magnitude of the stake, but because they had scruples about betting at all under such conditions.

Seven o'clock struck, and they suggested that Mr. Fogg should go home and prepare for his journey.

" I am always ready," replied that cool gentleman as he continued to deal. " Diamonds are trumps, Mr. Stuart; it is your lead."

CHAPTER IV

Phileas Fogg astonishes Passepartout, his servant

At twenty-five minutes past seven, Phileas Fogg, having won twenty guineas, took leave of his friends and left the Reform Club. At seven-fifty he opened the street-door of his house and entered.

Passepartout, who had studied his programme conscientiously, was very much surprised to see his master, for, according to precedent, he was not due until midnight.

Phileas Fogg walked straight up to his room and called Passepartout.

Passepartout did not reply. The summons could not be addressed to him. It was not time.

" Passepartout," cried Mr. Fogg again, but without raising his voice.

Passepartout went upstairs.

" I have called you twice," said Mr. Fogg.

" It is not midnight yet," replied Passepartout, holding out his watch.

" I know that," replied Phileas Fogg. " I don't blame you. We shall start in ten minutes for Dover and Calais."

The Frenchman grimaced; he evidently did not understand.

"Are you going to leave, sir?" he said.

"Yes," replied his master, "we are going round the world."

Passepartout opened his eyes to their utmost extent, and looked the picture of stupid astonishment.

"Around the world?" he repeated.

"In eighty days," replied Mr. Fogg, "so we have no time to lose."

"But the luggage?" said Passepartout, who was wagging his head to and fro in an imbecile manner.

"We want no luggage. We only require a carpet-bag. Pack up a couple of nightshirts and some socks for each of us; we can buy what we want *en route*. Take my mackintosh and travelling cloak and some thick boots, though we shall not walk much. Look sharp!"

Passepartout wished to speak, but could not. He left Mr. Fogg's bedroom and ascended to his own. Throwing himself into a chair, he exclaimed:

"Well, this is coming it pretty strong. Here am I who wanted to be quiet, now——"

He rose without finishing his sentence, and mechanically set about making preparations for his departure. Round the world in eighty days! Was his master a lunatic? No; it must be a joke; they were going to Dover very likely, perhaps to Calais, but that he did not object to, for he had not seen his native country for five years. They might even go so far as Paris, and he would have no objection to see the capital once again, but certainly a gentleman so careful of his steps would stop there; but, on the other hand, it was undoubtedly true that this same gentleman was leaving his home, and who could tell what he might do?

At eight o'clock Passepartout had packed the

carpet-bag, and in a very disturbed state of mind he went downstairs.

Mr. Fogg was quite ready. Under his arm he carried *Bradshaw's Continental Guide*. He took the little bag from Passepartout, and, opening it, put in a bulky roll of bank-notes, which will pass anywhere.

" You have not forgotten anything?" he said.

" No, sir."

" My mackintosh and cloak?"

" Here they are."

" Good. Take the bag, and take care of it, for there are twenty thousand pounds in it."

Passepartout nearly let it fall, as if it had been weighted with twenty thousand pounds in gold.

Then the master and servant descended together. The street-door was shut and double-locked by Mr. Fogg. A cab was called from the rank and they drove to Charing Cross, the station of the South-Eastern Railway.

It was twenty minutes past eight when they reached the terminus. Passepartout jumped out. Mr. Fogg paid the cabman.

Just then a poor beggar-woman, carrying a child in her arms, and looking very tattered and miserable, wearing a ragged shawl, and without shoes or stockings, asked for alms.

Mr. Fogg took the twenty guineas he had won at whist from his pocket and gave them to her.

" Take these, my good woman," he said, " I am glad I have met you."

He then went into the station.

Passepartout felt the tears come into his eyes as he witnessed his master's liberality. Mr. Fogg had risen in his estimation.

They entered the waiting-room together. Phileas Fogg told Passepartout to take two tickets for Paris;

then, turning round, he perceived his five friends who had come to see him off.

" Well, gentlemen, I am about to start, and you will see by the *visas* on my passport when I return that I have performed the journey."

" Oh, Mr. Fogg, that is not necessary. We will take your word for it," said Gauthier Ralph politely.

" That is all the better then," said Fogg.

" You won't forget when you are due in London again," said Stuart.

" In eighty days," replied Mr. Fogg—" on Saturday the 21st of December, 1872, at a quarter to nine in the evening. *Au revoir*, gentlemen."

At twenty minutes to nine Phileas Fogg and his servant got into the train. At eight-forty-five the whistle sounded, and the train started.

The night was dark, and a fine rain was falling. Mr. Fogg, comfortably ensconced in his corner, made no remark. Passepartout, still half-dazed, mechanically clutched the bag containing the bank-notes.

But the train had not yet passed Sydenham when Passepartout uttered a cry of despair.

" What is the matter with you?" said Mr. Fogg.

" I—in my hurry I forgot——"

" What?"

" I forgot to turn the gas off in my room."

" Very well, my lad," replied Mr. Fogg quietly; " it will burn at your expense meantime."

CHAPTER V

A new investment on the London Stock Exchange

Phileas Fogg when he left London was pretty sure that his departure would create a sensation. The news of his wager spread from the club to newspaper reporters, and thus to all the newspapers in the kingdom.

The idea of going round the world was commented upon, discussed, and argued with as much ardour as the Alabama claims had been. Some took Mr. Fogg's part, but the majority opposed him. To accomplish his task in such a time was pronounced an impossibility, and with the means at his disposal it was madness.

The Times, the *Standard*, *Evening Star*, the *Morning Chronicle*, and twenty other papers, gave their verdict against Mr. Fogg. The *Daily Telegraph* only supported him in moderation. Phileas Fogg was looked upon, more or less, as a maniac, and his friends of the Reform Club were blamed for having taken the bet, which only betokened the madness of its proposer.

A series of extremely warm but logical articles were written on this question. The interest which the English take in everything pertaining to geography is well known. So readers of every class devoured any intelligence respecting Mr. Fogg's journey.

For a few days his cause was espoused by some bold spirits, principally women, more particularly when the *Illustrated London News* came out with his portrait. Some men said they did not see why he should not succeed: more extraordinary things had happened. These were principally readers of the *Daily Telegraph*, but it was evident that even that paper was beginning to change its views.

In fact, on the 7th of October a long article appeared in the *Proceedings* of the Royal Geographical Society which discussed the question in all its bearings, and conclusively demonstrated the futility of the whole proceeding. According to that article, everything physically and morally was opposed to him. To argue success a miraculous concordance of the time of the arrival and departure of steamers and trains must be conceded—a concordance which could not and did not exist. Perhaps in Europe he might count upon comparatively punctual service, but when three days are occupied in crossing India, and seven days in traversing the United States, how could he calculate upon the elements of success? Accidents to machinery, rails, collisions, or bad weather, were all against Phileas Fogg. Were not even steamers at the mercy of winds and fogs? and even the best of them may be delayed two or three days. Now one single day's delay might cut irreparably the chain of communication. If Phileas Fogg lost a steamer by a few hours only he would be obliged to wait for the next one, and that fact would imperil the success of the whole undertaking.

This article made a great noise; it was reproduced in all the papers, and Phileas Fogg's shares fell considerably.

For a few days after his departure a good deal was betted for or against his success. It is well known that the English are great gamblers; it is the British temperament; so not only did the members of the Reform Club lay considerable bets for or against Phileas Fogg, but the public went into the speculation. Phileas Fogg became a favourite; he had a value on the Stock Exchange; people speculated in Fogg, and he was offered at par or at a premium but five days after his departure, and on the appearance of the article in the Royal Geographical Society's *Proceedings*, the bonds went down; they were offered in bulk, and at last they went down from fifty to a hundred discount.

One supporter still remained faithful to him, and that was the paralysed old Lord Albemarle. This nobleman, who was unable to leave his armchair, would have given all he possessed to have gone round the world even in ten years. He had laid five thousand pounds on Phileas Fogg, and when people pointed out to him the absurdity and folly of the expedition he would reply:

" If the thing be feasible, Englishmen ought to be the first men to do it."

So the partisans of Phileas Fogg became fewer every day. Everybody was against him, and at last people would only take 150 or 200 to 1, and seven days after his departure an unexpected incident deprived him of any support whatever.

In fact, at nine o'clock that evening the inspector of police at Scotland Yard received the following telegram:

Suez to London

Rowan, Police Commissioner, Scotland Yard.

I have traced the bank robber, Phileas Fogg. Send warrant at once to Bombay.

Fix.

The effect of this dispatch was immediately visible. The honourable gentleman gave way to the bank robber. His photograph, deposited at the Reform Club with those of other members, was examined. It appeared to be a likeness of the man they sought. People now began to recollect Phileas Fogg's isolated and mysterious existence, his sudden departure, and it appeared evident that under the pretext of a journey round the world, and with the excuse of a ridiculous wager, he had no other object in view than to throw the English detectives off the scent.

CHAPTER VI

In which the Detective Fix betrays some natural impatience

The circumstances under which the telegram was dispatched are as follow:

On Wednesday, the 9th of October, at eleven o'clock in the morning, the P. & O. Company's steamer *Mongolia* was expected at Suez. She made the voyage from Brindisi to Bombay through the Suez Canal. Pending her arrival two men were walking up and down the quay amongst the natives and visitors who thronged the town, which is likely to increase in importance, thanks to M. de Lesseps' great work.

One of these two men was the English consul, who, in spite of the prophecies of the English Government and the sinister predictions of Stephenson the engineer, saw English ships passing through the Canal daily, and so shortening the route to India by one-half.

The other man was short and thin, with a nervously-twitching but intelligent face. His eyes sparkled brightly, but he could quench their ardour when he pleased. Just then, however, he was very impatient, and quite unable to keep still for a moment.

This was Fix, the English detective, one of the police-agents who had been sent to the various ports after the bank robbery had been committed. This Fix noticed every traveller who landed at Suez, and if any one of them resembled the culprit he would at once have been arrested pending the arrival of a warrant.

Fix had received the description of the culprit two days before. It was that of the distinguished and well-dressed person who had been seen at the Bank of England.

The detective was more particularly on the alert in consequence of the reward that had been offered, and was proportionately impatient for the arrival of the *Mongolia*.

" You say that the ship is not likely to be behind time?" remarked Fix to the consul.

" No," he replied; " she was signalled from Port Said yesterday, and the sixty kilometres through the

Canal are nothing to a vessel of her speed. I have told you already that the *Mongolia* has always gained the premium of twenty-five pounds given by the Government for every advance of four-and-twenty hours on the regulation time."

" She comes direct from Brindisi, I suppose?" said Fix.

" Yes; she takes the Indian mail there. She left Brindisi at five o'clock on Saturday afternoon, so have patience. She is sure to be here soon. But I do not see how, with the information you have received, you can recognize your man if he be on board the *Mongolia*."

" These sort of people are always discovered by instinct—by scent, so to speak. I have arrested more than one of these gentlemen in my life, and if the fellow be on board I will answer for it; the fellow will not escape me."

" I hope you may catch him, for he has made away with a large sum of money."

" A magnificent robbery!" replied the detective with enthusiasm—" fifty-five thousand pounds! We do not have such windfalls as that every day. Thieves are becoming ' funky.' The race of Jack Sheppard is dying out. Fellows get taken up now for a few shillings."

" Mr. Fix," replied the consul, " you speak like a man who deserves to succeed; but I tell you I think you will find your work has been cut out for you, for you know quite well that the description you have received may be that of a perfectly honest man."

" Great thieves always do resemble honest men," replied the detective dogmatically. " A scoundrelly-looking man would not have a chance; it is the honest physiognomy that we are obliged to unmask. It is difficult, I confess; it is more than business—it is art."

It is pretty evident that Fix had a good deal of self-reliance.

Meantime the quay got more animated. Sailors of different nationalities, porters, merchants, and fellahs, were all mingled. The steamer was evidently expected very soon.

The day was fine, but cool in consequence of the east wind. The pale sunlight lighted up the distant minarets of the town; to the south the long jetty extended like an arm into the roadstead of Suez. The surface of the Red Sea was dotted with boats of all descriptions.

Fix kept moving about the crowd scrutinizing the faces of the passers-by with a sort of professional habit.

It was then half-past ten o'clock.

" The steamer is not coming after all," he exclaimed as he heard the harbour-clock strike.

" She is not far off," said the consul.

" How long will she stop here?" asked Fix.

" Four hours to coal. From Suez to Aden is thirteen hundred and ten miles, so she must lay in a good supply."

" And from Suez I suppose she goes to Bombay?"

" Yes, direct, without breaking bulk."

" Well," said Fix, " if the thief has come by this boat he will probably land here so as to gain the Dutch or French possessions in Asia by some other route than through British territory in India, where he would not be safe."

" I don't expect he is a very sharp fellow," replied the consul. " An English thief is always safer in London."

This remark gave the detective food for thought, and the consul departed to his office. Fix, now left alone, became more impatient than ever. He had some presentiment that his man was on board the

Mongolia, and if the criminal had left England with the intention of reaching America, the route to India, being less observed or more difficult to watch than the Atlantic route, would naturally be preferred.

The detective was not left long to his thoughts. A series of shrill whistles announced the steamer's approach. The whole horde of porters and fellahs hurried along the quay in a manner very much to the detriment of the clothes of the lookers-on. A number of boats put off from the quay to meet the *Mongolia.*

The gigantic hull of the mail steamer soon appeared, and as the clock struck eleven she came to anchor in the roadstead, while a cloud of steam escaped from her safety-valve.

There were a great many passengers on board.

Some remained on the spar deck admiring the view, but the greater number came off in the boats which had gone out to meet the ship.

Fix scrutinized the faces of all those who landed.

As he was thus employed one of the passengers approached him, pushing aside all the fellahs who offered their services. He asked the detective to point him out the consul's office, at the same time producing his passport, to which he wished to have the British *visa* fixed.

Fix took the passport mechanically and glanced at it. His hands shook involuntarily when he perceived that the description of the owner of the passport was identical with that of the criminal he sought.

" This is not your passport," he said to the passenger.

" No, it is my master's."

" And where is your master?"

" On board the ship."

" Well, he must come on shore himself to establish his identity."

" Is that absolutely necessary?"

" Indispensable."

" Where is the consul's office?"

" Over there at the corner of the square," replied the detective, indicating a house about two hundred yards off.

" Well, I will go and tell my master, but he won't be best pleased at my disturbing him."

So saying, the passenger nodded to Fix and made his way back to the steamer.

CHAPTER VII

Showing the uselessness of passports where the police are concerned

The detective quickly went in the direction of the consul's office. He was immediately ushered into the presence of that official on the plea of urgent business.

Without any preamble he said, " I have every reason to believe that my man is on board the *Mongolia*," and then Fix related what had passed between the servant and himself respecting the passport.

" Very well, Mr. Fix," replied the consul: " I shall not be sorry to see the fellow myself, but I do not expect he will come here if things are as you say. A thief does not care to leave a trace, and, besides, there is no necessity to have the passport *visé*."

" If he be the man I take him to be he will come," replied the detective.

" To have his passport examined do you mean?"

" Yes. Passports are of no use except to trouble honest people and to favour the escape of rogues. I expect this fellow's passport will be all right, but I hope you will not *visé* it."

" Why not? If it be correct I have no right to refuse."

" Nevertheless I must try to keep the man here until I receive a warrant from London."

" Ah! that is your business, Mr. Fix. For my part——"

The consul did not finish his sentence, and a knock at the door was heard and two strangers were admitted, one of whom was the servant who had met the detective on the quay.

The new-comers were, in fact, Mr. Fogg and Passepartout; the former presented his passport, and quietly requested the consul to add his *visa*.

The consul took the document and read it attentively, while Fix, from a corner, examined the stranger narrowly.

When the consul had finished reading he turned and said:

" You are Mr. Phileas Fogg, I presume?"

" Yes," replied that gentleman.

" And this man is your servant?"

" Yes—a Frenchman named Passepartout."

" You have come from London?"

" Yes."

" And you are bound?"

" To Bombay."

" Very well. You know that this formality is useless; the production of the passport only is necessary."

" I know that," replied Fogg, " but I wanted you to testify to my appearance here."

" Very well," replied the consul, who at once signed the passport. Fogg paid the fees, and, bowing coldly, left, followed by his servant.

" Well?" said the detective.

" Well," replied the consul, " he appears to me to be perfectly honest."

" Very likely," replied Fix, " but that is not the point. Do you not see that this gentleman answers exactly to the description of the thief?"

" So far I agree with you, but all descriptions——"

" I will put the thing to rights," replied Fix; " the servant appears to be less unapproachable than his master, and besides, being a Frenchman, he can't help talking. I will soon return, sir."

As he spoke the detective left the office and went in search of Passepartout.

Meanwhile Mr. Fogg having left the consul's house went down to the quay; there he gave some orders to his servant, and then went on board the *Mongolia* and to his cabin. There he took out his note-book and made the following entries:

Left London, Wednesday, October 2nd, 8.45 p.m.

Arrived in Paris, Thursday, October 3rd, 7.20 a.m.

Left Paris, Thursday, 8.40 a.m.

Reached Turin viâ Mont Cenis, Friday, October 4th, 6.35 a.m.

Left Turin, Friday, 7.20 a.m.

Arrived at Brindisi, Saturday, October 5th, 4 p.m.

Embarked on *Mongolia*, Saturday, 5 p.m.

Arrived at Suez, Wednesday, October 9th, 11 a.m.

Total hours occupied, $158\frac{1}{2}$, or $6\frac{1}{2}$ days

Mr. Fogg wrote this down in a journal ruled in columns, from the 2nd of October to the 21st of December, which indicated the month, the day of the month, and the day of the week, and the days at which he was due at the principal points in his route—for instance, Paris, Brindisi, Suez, Bombay, Calcutta, Singapore, Hong Kong, Yokohama, San Francisco, New York, Liverpool, London; and there was also a column in which the time gained or the loss experienced in each place might be noted.

This methodical itinerary would show Mr. Fogg in a moment whether he was ahead or behind his time.

On that day, October 9th, he noted his arrival at Suez, and saw that he had neither gained nor lost anything.

A3—C

Then he breakfasted in his cabin; he never thought of going to look at the town, as he was one of those Englishmen who see foreign countries with the eyes of their servants.

CHAPTER VIII

In which Passepartout talks a little too much

Fix soon rejoined Passepartout, who was staring about him on the quay, endeavouring to see all he could.

" Well, my friend," said Fix, " so your passport has been *viséd* all right?"

" Ah, is it you?" replied the Frenchman. " Yes, we are all right, thank you."

" And you are now seeing what you can?"

" Yes, but we are going so quickly that the journey seems to me like a dream. And so we are actually in Suez?"

" Yes, in Suez."

" In Egypt?"

" In Egypt decidedly."

" And in Africa?"

" Yes."

" In Africa! I can scarcely believe it," replied Passepartout. " Just fancy that I had not the faintest idea that we should go beyond Paris, and I saw nothing of the city except between seven-twenty and eight-forty a.m., between the railway stations, as we drove from one to the other through the rain. I am very sorry. I should have been glad to have seen once more Père la Chaise and the circus in the Champs-Elysées."

" You are in a very great hurry, I suppose?" said Fix.

" I? Oh dear no, it is my master. By the way, I must buy some shirts and shoes. He came away with scarcely any luggage."

" I will take you to a shop where you will find all that is necessary."

" You are really very kind," replied Passepartout.

So they started off together, Passepartout chattering all the time.

" But I must take good care I do not lose the steamer," he said.

" You have time," said Fix; " it is scarcely twelve o'clock."

Passepartout drew out his great watch.

" Twelve o'clock! It is only fifty-two minutes past nine."

" Your watch is slow," replied Fix.

" My watch slow! My family watch, which has descended to me from my grandfather! It never varies five minutes in a year. It is a perfect chronometer."

" I see what it is," said Fix; " you keep London time, which is about two hours slower than Suez time. You ought to set your watch at twelve o'clock in every country you pass through."

" I alter my watch!" said Passepartout. " Never!"

" Well, it will not agree with the sun, then."

" All the worse for the sun; it will be wrong," and then the lad put back his watch into his pocket with an indescribable air.

Shortly afterwards Fix said:

" You must have left London very hurriedly?"

" I should think so. Last Wednesday, at eight o'clock, contrary to all his habits, Mr. Fogg came home from his club, and three-quarters of an hour after we were *en route*."

" Where is your master going?"

" Right round the world."

" Round the world?" exclaimed Fix.

" Yes, in eighty days. He says it is a wager, but I do not believe that. It does not stand to reason."

" Mr. Fogg is a character, I should think?"

" I believe you."

" He is very rich, I suppose?"

" He must be. He carries a tremendous sum with him, all in notes; he spares no expense. Just think : he promised a reward to the engineer of the *Mongolia* if he reached Bombay ahead of time."

" Have you been long with your master?"

" I only entered his service the very day we left."

One can imagine the effect these answers had upon the detective's suspicious nature. The precipitate departure from London so soon after the robbery, the money all in bank-notes, the anxiety to reach distant countries under pretext of a bet, all confirmed Fix in his idea. He still wished to talk to the Frenchman, and to make sure that he knew no more about his master than he had confessed, but at the same time Fix was certain that Phileas Fogg would not land at Suez, and that he was really going to Bombay.

" Is it far to Bombay?" asked Passepartout.

" Yes, some distance—about ten days' steaming."

" Where do you say Bombay is?"

" In India."

" In Asia?"

" Naturally."

" The devil! I was going to tell you. There is something on my mind—my burner."

" What burner?"

" The gas-burner, which I forgot, and which is still alight at my expense. I have reckoned that it costs me two shillings every four-and-twenty hours; that is just sixpence more than my wages, so you see the longer the journey is prolonged——"

It is not likely that Fix cared about the gas; he was not listening, for he had already made up his mind. He and the Frenchman had now reached the bazaar, where Fix left his companion to make his purchases, and hurried back to the consul's office, while he recommended Passepartout not to miss the *Mongolia*.

Now that the detective's suspicions were confirmed he regained all his coolness, and he said to the consul:

" I have not the slightest doubt that this is the man who wants to pass himself off as an eccentric person who wishes to go round the world in eighty days."

" Ah, he is pretty sharp, for he expects to return to London, having thrown the detectives of two continents off the scent."

" We shall soon see," replied Fix.

" Are you sure you are not mistaken?" said the consul again.

" I am sure I am not."

" Well, why should he be so anxious to have his passport *viséd* at Suez?"

" Why? Well, I do not know, but listen to me "; and in a few words he told the consul what Passepartout had communicated.

" Appearances are certainly against him," replied the consul. " What are you going to do?"

" I am going to wire to London for a warrant to arrest him at Bombay. I shall embark on the *Mongolia* and look after my man till we reach India, and there, on British territory, I shall arrest him."

So saying the agent took leave of the consul, and went to the telegraph-office where he dispatched the telegram we have already seen.

A quarter of an hour later Mr. Fix, small bag in hand, and plenty of money in his pocket, went on board the *Mongolia*, which soon afterwards steamed away at full speed down the Red Sea.

CHAPTER IX

*The Red Sea and the Indian Ocean are favourable to
Phileas Fogg*

The distance between Suez and Aden is exactly thirteen hundred and ten miles, and the steamers are
allowed one hundred and thirty-eight hours to accomplish it. The *Mongolia*, whose fires were fully fed,
appeared likely to do it in advance of time.

The greater part of the passengers from Brindisi
were bound for India viâ Bombay, for since the
railway has crossed the Peninsula it has not been
necessary to go round Point de Galle.

Amongst the passengers on board the *Mongolia*
were civil and military officers of every grade. Of the
former were representatives of the Imperial as well as
the Indian army holding lucrative appointments, so
life on board the *Mongolia* was very pleasant, including as it did many young Englishmen who, with
plenty of money, were going out to inaugurate branch
houses of business. The purser, almost as big a man
as the captain, feasted them well. There was breakfast in the morning, lunch at two o'clock, dinner at
half-past five, and supper at eight o'clock, and the
tables groaned under the dishes supplied by the ship's
commissariat. The lady passengers changed their
dresses twice a day, and there was music and dancing
whenever the weather was fine.

But the Red Sea, like all long and narrow gulfs, is
very capricious. When the wind blew broadside on
the *Mongolia* rolled tremendously; at those times the
ladies disappeared, the pianos were silent, singing and
dancing ceased for a time, but nevertheless the steamer
ploughed her way rapidly towards the straits of Babel-
Mandeb.

What was Phileas Fogg doing all this time? One

might easily fancy how anxious he was respecting the effects of the wind on the speed of the ship, that he was preoccupied respecting the machinery, or any accident that might compromise the success of his undertaking; but if he was anxious he never permitted his anxiety to be seen; he was as imperturbable as ever; no accident could put him out. He did not appear to be more interested than one of the chronometers; he was rarely seen on deck; he did not care to observe the Red Sea, which is so full of interest, and the scene of one of the most remarkable events in the history of the human race. He never came up to look at the curious towns on its banks, he never troubled himself about the dangers of this Arabian gulf, respecting which so many ancient historians have written, and upon which sailors in former days never dared to embark without first offering a propitiatory sacrifice.

How did this " original " amuse himself on board the *Mongolia*? For in the first place he ate his four meals a day regularly, for no rolling or pitching had the least effect upon his organization. And then he played whist.

Yes, he had met some people as enthusiastic as himself—a tax-collector, on his way to Goa; the Reverend Decimus Smith, who was returning to Bombay; and an English brigadier-general, who was about to join his corps at Benares—these three passengers were as fond of whist as Mr. Fogg himself, and passed hours at play in silence.

As for Passepartout, he having escaped sea-sickness also ate his meals conscientiously, and under these circumstances rather enjoyed the voyage. He had made up his mind to see the country while he enjoyed his meals, and was sure all this would come to an end at Bombay.

On the 10th of October, the day after they left Suez,

Passepartout was agreeably surprised to meet on deck the same gentleman who had been so polite to him in Egypt.

" Surely," he said, " I have the pleasure of meeting the gentleman who so kindly assisted me at Suez?"

" Oh yes," replied the detective, " I recognize you now. Are you not the servant of that eccentric Englishman?"

" Just so, Mr.——"

" Fix."

" Mr. Fix," continued Passepartout, " I am delighted to see you. Where are you going to?"

" To Bombay, like yourself."

" All the better. Have you ever made this voyage before?"

" Oh dear yes," replied Fix, " I am one of the company's agents."

" Then you know India very well?"

" Well, yes," replied Fix, who did not wish to say too much.

" India is a curious place, is it not?"

" Very curious: there are mosques, minarets, temples, fakirs, pagodas, tigers, serpents, dancing girls; but I hope you will have time to see the country."

" I hope so too, Mr. Fix. It can scarcely be expected that one will not be able to do more than to jump from a steamer into a train, and from the train to another steamer, under the pretext of going round the world in eighty days. No, all these gymnastics will cease at Bombay I hope."

" Is Mr. Fogg quite well?" asked Mr. Fix politely.

" Quite well; so am I. I eat like an ogre. It is the sea air, I suppose."

" I never see your master on deck, though."

" Never; he has no curiosity."

" Do you know, M. Passepartout, that this pretended voyage round the world has very likely a secret meaning—some diplomatic mission, for instance?"

" I assure you, Mr. Fix, I know nothing about it; and to tell you the truth I would not give half-a-crown to know."

After this meeting Passepartout and Fix often talked together, the detective doing all in his power to draw Passepartout out. He would often treat him to a glass of whisky or beer, which the valet accepted without ceremony, and even reciprocated, all the time pronouncing the detective to be a perfect gentleman.

Meantime the steamer made good way. On the 13th, Mocha, surrounded by its ruined walls, was sighted. Beyond, in the mountains, were immense coffee plantations. Passepartout was delighted to see this celebrated town, and likened it and its ruined walls to an immense cup and saucer.

During the following night the *Mongolia* passed through the Strait of Babel-Mandeb, which is called by the Arabs the Gate of Tears, and on the 14th they made Steamer Point, to the north-west of Aden, where they were to coal.

It is an important business this coaling, particularly so far from the mines, and it costs the P. & O. Company £800,000 a year. It is necessary to establish depots in many places in distant seas, and the coal costs more than £3 a ton.

The *Mongolia* had still sixteen hundred and fifty miles to make before reaching Bombay, and was obliged to stop four hours at Steamer Point to coal.

But this delay did not affect Phileas Fogg's programme. It had been foreseen. Besides, the *Mongolia* had reached Aden on the morning of the 14th instead of the 15th, when she was due, so there was a gain of about fifteen hours.

Mr. Fogg and his servant went on shore to have the passport *viséd*. Fix followed them unnoticed. Mr. Fogg, having gone through this formality, returned on board to his interrupted game of whist.

Passepartout, according to his habit, wandered about in the crowd of Somanlis, Banians, Parsees, Jews, Arabs, and Europeans which make up the twenty-five thousand inhabitants of Aden. He admired the fortifications of the Indian Seas, and the magnificent cisterns, at which the English engineers were still at work two thousand years after the engineers of King Solomon.

" This is all very curious," said Passepartout to himself as he went on board. " I see that travelling is useful if one wishes to have new ideas."

At six o'clock in the evening the *Mongolia* started again. She had now one hundred and sixty-eight hours to reach Bombay. The weather was good and the wind favourable, so the sails were hoisted to assist the screw.

The ship was steadier, so the ladies reappeared on deck, and dancing and singing began again. The voyage was most favourable, and Passepartout was delighted with his pleasant companion Fix.

About midday on Sunday, the 20th of October, they sighted the Indian coast. Two hours later the pilot came on board, a long range of hills was soon visible, and palm-trees were distinguished. At length the steamer ran into the roads formed by the isles of Salcette, Colaba, Elephanta, and Butcher, and at half-past four brought up alongside the quay.

Phileas Fogg was just finishing his thirty-third rubber that day. He and his partner had scored a treble, and terminated the voyage successfully.

The *Mongolia* was not due till the 22nd, but as she had arrived in Bombay on the 20th, Mr. Fogg had gained two days, which he entered methodically on the credit side of his account.

CHAPTER X

Passepartout is lucky in escaping with the loss of his shoes only

Everybody knows that the Indian Peninsula includes a superficial area of 1,400,000 square miles, upon which is irregularly distributed a population of 180,000,000. The British Government is absolute over the greater portion of this country. The Governor-General lives in Calcutta, and the deputies at Madras, Bombay, and Bengal has its Lieutenant-Governor at Agra.

But British India, properly so called, only includes 700,000 square miles, with a population of 100,000,000 or 110,000,000, so there is still an immense proportion of territory under native rule, and in the interior is governed by fierce and absolute rajahs.

Since 1756, when the first British settlement was established at Madras, till the Sepoy Mutiny in 1857, the East India Company was all-powerful. It by degrees annexed various provinces or purchased them, and maintained its own army, but now it no longer exists, and the British possessions in India belong to the Crown.

Thus the aspect, manners, and ethnographical divisions of the peninsula alter daily. Formerly travelling was carried on by a most antique means of transport, but now steamers plough the Indus and the Ganges, and railways have formed a network throughout the country.

The course of the railway does not cut across India direct. As the crow flies the distance is only eleven hundred miles, and the trains ought not to take more than three days to accomplish the distance; but the loop to Allahabad lengthens it by a third.

The Great Indian Peninsular Railway runs as follows: Leaving Bombay Island it crosses Salcette to the mainland at Tamiat, crosses the Ghauts, thence turns to the north-east at Burhampoor, skirts the territory of Bundelcund, and so ascends to Allahabad, then, turning to the east, it strikes the Ganges at Benares, and then the line descends in a south-easterly direction, by Burdivan and the French town of Chandernagor, to the terminus at Calcutta.

It was half-past four p.m. when the passengers from the *Mongolia* landed at Bombay, and the train for Calcutta started at eight precisely.

Mr. Fogg took leave of his partners and left the steamer, giving his servant orders respecting a few purchases, and enjoining upon him the necessity to be at the station before eight o'clock, he went to the consul's bureau.

He did not care to see any of the "lions" of Bombay —the library, the docks, the fortifications, nor the cotton market, the mosques and bazaars, the churches, the splendid pagoda on Malabar Hill, nor the Elephanta Caves, etc. No. He went quietly from the consul's office to the railway station and ordered his dinner.

Amongst other dishes the landlord recommended a certain "rabbit of the country." Phileas Fogg accepted the dainty, but found it disgusting, and rang the bell. The landlord appeared.

"Sir," said he, "do you call this a rabbit?"

"Yes, my lord," replied the landlord, "a jungle rabbit."

"Do you think that rabbit mewed when you killed it?"

"Mewed! Oh, my lord, I swear to you——"

44

"My good sir," said Mr. Fogg coldly, "you need not swear, but please to remember that cats used to be considered sacred in this country. I am afraid those happy days have passed."

"For the cats, my lord?"

"Perhaps also for travellers," replied Mr. Fogg as he continued his dinner.

Mr. Fix landed shortly after Mr. Fogg, and he too went first to the consul's office. He introduced himself as a detective, told the object of his mission and how matters stood. He inquired if any warrant had been received.

No, it had not come, and it was impossible it could have arrived just yet.

Fix was much disappointed. He wished to have obtained a warrant on the spot, but it was refused; the authorities at Bombay had no power to grant such an instrument. This rigorous observance of rules is perfectly in accordance with English red-tapeism.

Fix did not insist, and saw that he would have to wait the arrival of the warrant, but he made up his mind not to lose sight of the robber. He had no doubt that Phileas Fogg would remain some time in Bombay at least, for that was Passepartout's conviction, and meantime the warrant would probably arrive.

But it was now evident to Passepartout that his master intended to leave Bombay as quickly as he had left Suez and Paris. He saw that the journey was not to end at any rate till they reached Calcutta, and perhaps not then. The servant began to think that, after all, perhaps his master's explanation of the wager was a true one, and that, notwithstanding his own love of repose, he would be obliged to rush round the world in eighty days.

In the meantime, and after having purchased some

45

shirts and shoes, Passepartout walked about the streets.
There were numbers of people of all races promenad-
ing, Persians, Armenians, Parsees, and Europeans of
all nationalities, for it was a Parsee festival, directed to
be held by the votaries of Zoroaster. These Parsees
are the most intelligent, civilized, and austere of the
Hindoo races, and to this sect the richest native Bombay merchants belonged. On this occasion a sort of
religious carnival was being celebrated. There were
processions and dances, in which gaudily-clad baya-
deres took part to the sound of viols and tomtoms.

Passepartout was delighted and astonished at all
these curious ceremonies, but unfortunately for him
and his master he imperilled the whole object of his
master's journey.

After having watched the Parsee carnival he went
towards the railway station, but passing the pagoda on
Malabar Hill he thought he would enter.

He was ignorant of two things—firstly, that pagodas
are forbidden to Christians; and, secondly, even
believers may only go in if they leave their shoes at the
door, and the British Government respects the sanctity
of the native mosques, severely punishing anyone who
violates them.

But Passepartout, like any other ignorant tourist,
walked in, and before long found himself sprawling
on his back on the sacred pavement. Three priests
with furious glances rushed upon him, tore off his
shoes, and began to pommel him soundly, screaming
savagely all the time.

The vigorous and agile Frenchman soon jumped up
again. With a blow and a well-directed kick he upset
two of his adversaries, who were encumbered by their
long robes, and then, darting out of the temple, he
quickly outdistanced the other priest and evaded him
in the crowd.

46

At five minutes to eight o'clock he arrived at the railway station without his hat and shoes, and minus the parcel.

Fix was on the platform. Having followed Mr. Fogg, he saw that he was about to quit Bombay. The detective made up his mind to go to Calcutta at any rate, and farther if necessary. Passepartout did not see Fix, who kept in the shade, but Fix heard Passepartout's narrative of what had occurred.

" I hope you won't behave this way again," said Phileas Fogg simply as he entered the carriage.

Passepartout, with naked feet, stepped in, crest-fallen and silent.

Fix was just about to get into another compartment when an idea struck him, and he turned back.

" No, I will remain," he thought; " an offence has been committed on Indian territory. I have him now."

At that moment the engine whistled loudly, and the train moved out of the station.

CHAPTER XI

Phileas Fogg buys a " mount " at a fabulous price

The train started punctually, taking the usual variety of travellers of all classes. Passepartout occupied the same compartment as his master. A third traveller was in the opposite corner; this was Brigadier-General Sir Francis Cromarty, one of Mr. Fogg's partners at whist between Suez and Bombay, and who was now on his way to join his regiment at Benares.

Sir Francis Cromarty was a tall, fair man, about fifty years old, who had distinguished himself greatly in the Indian Mutiny. He had lived in India for many years, and seldom went home on leave. He was extremely well informed respecting Indian habits and customs, and would gladly have imparted any information to Mr. Fogg had he asked for it; but that gentleman did nothing of the kind, for he never really travelled, he merely "made tracks." He was a heavy body describing an orbit according to mechanical laws. At that very moment he was reckoning how many hours had passed since he had left London, and had he been a demonstrative man he would have rubbed his hands with delight.

Sir Francis Cromarty had already noticed Mr. Fogg's eccentricity on board ship, and wondered whether he possessed a heart beneath that cold envelope, and whether Phileas Fogg had a soul sensible to the beauties of Nature or to moral aspirations. The gallant general was puzzled; he had never met an orginal like Mr. Fogg.

But Mr. Fogg had not hidden the purpose nor the conditions of his journey from Sir Francis. The general saw nothing in it but the absurdity of its surroundings and the absence of the *transire benefaciendo* which ought to guide any reasonable man. At this rate this original gentleman would leave the world without having done any good for himself or his fellow-creatures.

An hour after the train left Bombay across the viaduct of Salcette to the continent. At Callyan Station they proceeded on the main line to Pauwell. At this point they entered the gorge of the Western Ghauts, the highest summits of which are crowned with trees.

From time to time Sir Francis and Phileas Fogg exchanged a few words, and the general remarked:

"Some years ago, Mr. Fogg, you would have experienced a decided check here which would have compromised your journey."

"How so, Sir Francis?"

"Because the railroad then ceased at the base of these mountains, and you would have had to travel in a palanquin or on a pony as far as Kandallah on the opposite side."

"The delay would have made no difference to me," replied Mr. Fogg. "I have provided against certain eventualities."

"Nevertheless you nearly came to grief in consequence of your servant's misadventure."

Passepartout was then fast asleep, his feet wrapped up in a railway-rug, and quite unconscious that he was referred to.

"The British Government is extremely severe upon such offenders, and rightly so," continued Sir Francis. "It is held that the religious scruples of the natives should be particularly respected, so if your servant had been arrested——"

"Well, supposing he had," replied Fogg, "he might have been condemned and punished, and returned quietly to Europe afterwards; but there was no reason why I should have been retarded."

There the conversation ceased for a time. During the night the train crossed the Ghauts, passed Nassik, and next day, the 21st of October, it crossed the comparatively flat territory of Khandish. The country was well cultivated and dotted with villages, above which the pagoda rose up in place of the European spire. Numerous rivulets, the greater number affluents of the Godavery, irrigated the country.

When Passepartout woke he looked about him, and could not believe that he was crossing India in a train. It was almost incredible, but it was true nevertheless. The engine, driven by an English engineer and lubricated with English oil, puffed out its smoke over coffee, cotton, and other plantations. The smoke curled in spirals around the groups of palms, amongst which picturesque bungalows could be perceived, and here and there were viharis, a sort of abandoned monasteries, and temples enriched with all the grace of Indian architecture. Then immense tracts of country were crossed, and jungles in which serpents and tigers fled at the screaming of the train, and finally through forests the abode of huge elephants, which watched the carriages pensively as they passed.

During the morning the train passed Malligaum and the blood-stained territory beyond it, sacred to the votaries of the goddess Kâli. Not far off was Ellora and its splendid pagodas, the celebrated Aurungabad, the capital of the fierce Aureng-Zeb, now a tributary of the Nizam. It was in this district that Feringhea, the chief of the Thugs, the king of stranglers, exercised his dominion. These assassins, united in a secret association, used to strangle in honour of the goddess of death victims of all ages without spilling blood, and in time there was scarcely a place where a corpse might not be found. The English Government has been very successful in putting down these murders, but the horrible association still exists and pursues its dreaded occupation.

At half-past twelve the train stopped at Burhampoor, and Passepartout was able to buy a pair of slippers, which, being ornamented with pearls, he wore with evident vanity.

The travellers breakfasted quickly, and crossing the river Tapty, a little stream which falls into the Gulf of Cambay, near Surat, the train speeded for Assurghur.

It may be as well that we should now analyse Passepartout's reflections. Till he reached Bombay he thought he would not have to proceed farther, but now that he was crossing India at full speed he saw things differently. His natural feelings revived; the fantastic ideas of his youth rose within him once more.

He accepted his master's projects and the story of the wager: the tour of the world to be made in eighty days, and which must not be exceeded. Already he was beginning to worry himself about possible accidents *en route*; he was beginning to feel interested in the wager, and trembled to think how nearly he had compromised the whole affair by his stupidity; so being much less phlegmatic than Mr. Fogg, he was more restless. He counted and re-counted the days, cursed the stoppages of the train, found fault with the pace, and in his heart found fault with Mr. Fogg for not having "tipped" the engine-driver. He quite forgot that a railroad is different from a steamboat; on the former the speed is regulated and the time fixed.

Towards evening the train entered the passes of the Sutpore Mountains, which divide the territory of Khandish from Bundelcund.

Next morning, the 22nd of October, Passepartout replied to Francis Cromarty's question as to the time by saying it was three o'clock in the morning, but as a matter of fact it was nearly four hours slow, as it was regulated by Greenwich meridian, which was nearly 77 degrees West.

Sir Francis corrected the time announced by Passepartout as Fix had done before him. The general tried to convince the man that he ought to regulate his watch by every new meridian, and as he was continually going east—that is to say, towards the sun— the days would become four minutes shorter by every degree. But it was useless; whether Passepartout understood or not, he did not alter his watch. It was an innocent fancy of his at any rate, and hurt nobody.

At eight in the morning, at about fifteen miles from Rothal Station, the train stopped, and the guard called out:

"All change here!"

Phileas Fogg and Sir Francis Cromarty looked at each other. They evidently did not understand this stoppage in the midst of a forest.

Passepartout, not less surprised, jumped out and returned almost immediately with the information that there was no railway beyond that point.

"What do you mean?" inquired Sir Francis.

"I mean that the train goes no farther."

The general, followed by Mr. Fogg, immediately descended. They both spoke to the guard.

"Where are we?" asked Sir Francis.

"At Kholby," replied the conductor.

"Why do we stop here?"

"Because the line is not finished beyond."

"How?—not finished?"

"No, there are still about fifty miles to be laid between this and Allahabad."

"The newspapers say that the railway is open throughout."

"I cannot help that, sir; they are mistaken."

"But you issue through tickets from Bombay to Calcutta," continued Sir Francis, who was beginning to get angry.

"No doubt," replied the guard, "but it is on the understanding that passengers provide their own transport from Kholby to Allahabad."

Sir Francis Cromarty was furious. Passepartout felt he would like to fight the guard; he did not dare to look at his master.

"Sir Francis," said Mr. Fogg, "as we must get on, do you not think we had better look for some conveyance?"

"I am afraid this delay will upset all your arrangements," replied Sir Francis.

"No," returned Fogg coolly, "it has all been foreseen."

"What! did you know that the line was interrupted?"

"Hardly; but I knew that I should be detained somewhere sooner or later. I have lost nothing yet. I have two days in hand. The steamer does not leave Calcutta for Hong Kong till noon on the 25th, this is only the 22nd, and we shall reach Calcutta in plenty of time."

There was nothing to say to such complete assurance as this.

It was only too true that the railway went no farther. Newspaper writers are very fond of anticipating matters, and they had prematurely announced the opening of the line. Most of the passengers knew it was not finished, and as soon as they left the train they hired all available modes of conveyance, so Mr. Fogg and Sir Francis Cromarty sought in vain for a vehicle.

"I shall walk," said Phileas Fogg.

Passepartout, when he heard this, grimaced eloquently at his magnificent but very thin slippers. Fortunately he had made a discovery, and he said timidly to his master:

"I think, sir, I have found a means of conveyance."

"What is it?"

"An elephant belonging to a native who lives near."

"Let us go and see this elephant," replied Mr. Fogg.

Five minutes later the three men reached a little hut surrounded by palisades. In the hut was a native, in the inclosure was an elephant, and at their request the former introduced the travellers to the latter.

They found this animal partly domesticated, as he had been trained for fighting purposes, not for work. With this object his master had begun to change the beast's naturally good disposition by feeding him on sugar and butter up to the pitch of fury known by the Hindoos as "mutch." This treatment would not appear the best for the purpose, but it is employed successfully. Fortunately for Mr. Fogg, this particular elephant had not yet developed any symptoms of " mutch."

Kiouni—for that was the beast's name—was, no doubt, quite able to travel for a long time at a rapid pace, and in default of any other conveyance Phileas Fogg resolved to employ him.

But elephants are dear in India, where they are becoming scarce. The males, which only are suitable for circus entertainments, are much sought after. The animals rarely breed when in captivity, so they have to be procured by hunting. This will explain why, when Mr. Fogg offered to hire the animal, the owner refused point blank.

Fogg persisted and offered ten pounds an hour, which was refused; twenty was again refused; forty pounds was declined. Passepartout jumped as each offer was made, but the Indian could not be tempted.

The sum was a large one nevertheless. Supposing that the elephant took fifteen hours to reach Allahabad he would earn six hundred pounds.

Mr. Fogg, as coolly as ever, then proposed to purchase the animal for a thousand pounds down.

Again the Indian declined; perhaps he thought he would get more.

Sir Francis took Mr. Fogg aside and begged him to reflect before bidding more. Mr. Fogg replied that he did not usually act without reflection; that a bet of twenty thousand pounds depended on it; that the elephant was necessary, and must be had, if he paid twenty times its value.

He then turned to the Indian again, whose little covetous eyes perceived that it was merely a matter of money. Phileas Fogg successively offered twelve hundred, fifteen hundred, eighteen hundred, and finally two thousand pounds. Passepartout's usually red face was now pale with emotion.

At the pressure of two thousand pounds the Indian yielded.

" By my new slippers that is a fine price for an elephant!" cried Passepartout.

This business concluded, they had only to find a guide. This was easy. A young and intelligent Parsee volunteered. Mr. Fogg accepted him and promised him a handsome remuneration, which, no doubt, would increase his intelligence.

The elephant was quickly equipped. The Parsee knew quite well the business of the mahout. He fixed a saddle on the elephant's back, and on each side he fastened a small howdah.

Phileas Fogg paid the Indian in bank-notes, which he took from his famous bag. Passepartout felt as if they were drawn from him by torture. Mr. Fogg then offered Sir Francis Cromarty a seat as far as Allahabad. The general accepted it. One traveller more or less made no difference to the elephant.

Provisions were then purchased. Sir Francis Cromarty took his place in one of the howdahs. Phileas Fogg occupied the other. Passepartout sat astride the saddle-cloth between them. The Parsee jerked himself up on the elephant's neck, and at nine o'clock they started, taking the shortest route through the thick forest.

CHAPTER XII

What happened to Phileas Fogg and his party as they traversed the forest

The guide, hoping to shorten the distance, left the railroad to the right, for it was carried circuitously through the Vindhai Mountains. The Parsee knew all the routes and by-paths, and as he said that twenty miles would be gained by cutting through the forest, they did as he wished.

Phileas Fogg and Sir Francis Cromarty, half buried in the howdahs, were very much shaken by the rough pace of the elephant, but they put up with the inconvenience in a truly British manner; they spoke little, and scarcely looked at each other.

Passepartout, who was seated on the back of the elephant, and had to endure all the inconvenience of the trotting, was very careful to obey his master's injunctions to keep his tongue within his teeth, or else it would have been bitten off. The brave lad was sometimes thrown upon the elephant's neck, sometimes upon his croup, and jumped up and down like a clown on a spring board, but he joked and laughed all the time, and even fed Kiouni with sugar, which the elephant took in his trunk without abating his regular trot for one moment.

After two hours' journey the guide gave the elephant a rest for an hour. After he had quenched his thirst, the animal made a meal of branches. Sir Francis did not complain of the delay, for he was very much bruised. Mr. Fogg did not appear at all the worse.

"He must be a man of iron," said the general, looking at his companion with admiration.

"Of hammered iron," replied Passepartout, who was preparing breakfast.

At midday they started again. The country was very wild. To the forest succeeded groves of dates and palms, then vast arid plains dotted with bushes and great blocks of syenite. All this portion of Bundelcund is seldom traversed, and is inhabited by a fanatical population who practise the most horrible Hindoo rites. The authority of the Indian Government is scarcely recognized; the whole country is under the influence of the rajahs, who are very difficult to be got at amongst their mountain retreats.

Bands of ferocious Indians were frequently noticed who made angry signs as they perceived the rapidly-trotting elephant passing by, and besides, the Parsee took care to avoid these people. Very few animals were seen, even monkeys were scarce, and they fled with a thousand grimaces and contortions, which amused Passepartout greatly.

One thing particularly troubled that young man; this was how Mr. Fogg would dispose of the elephant when he got to Allahabad; would he take it with him? That was not likely. The expense of the carriage of such an animal would be enormous. Would he sell it or set him free? There was no doubt that such an estimable animal required some consideration. Even if Mr. Fogg were to make him (Passepartout) a present of the animal it would embarrass him extremely. These considerations occupied Passepartout very much.

At eight o'clock p.m. they had cleared the mountains, and the travellers halted at a ruined bungalow at a southern slope.

They had now come about twenty-five miles with the elephant, and had still about the same distance to reach Allahabad. The night was rather chilly, so the Parsee lit a fire in the bungalow which was very welcome, and the travellers ate their frugal supper from the provisions they purchased at Kholby. The conversation, never very lively, soon gave way to snores. The guide kept watch beside Kiouni, who slept outside under a tree.

Nothing happened during the night. Now and then the growling of the panthers and other animals broke the silence, but they did not disturb the

57

occupants of the bungalow. Sir Francis Cromarty slept like a British officer who had done his duty. Passepartout was restless, and seemed to be riding the elephant in his sleep. Mr. Fogg slept as quietly as if he had been in his bed in Savile Row.

At six in the morning they started once more. The guide hoped to reach Allahabad that evening, so that Mr. Fogg, in that case, would only have lost a portion of the forty-eight hours he had in reserve.

They descended the last slopes of the Vindhias. Kiouni had continued his rapid pace. About midday they passed Kallanger, on the Cani, one of the little affluents of the Ganges. They avoided as much as possible all the villages, and felt more secure in doing so. Allahabad was now only twelve miles to the north-east, so the party halted in a grove of bananas, the fruit of which is as wholesome as bread and as succulent as cream, and was highly appreciated by the travellers.

At two o'clock they entered a dense forest which extended for many miles. The guide preferred to travel in the shade of the woods, but in any case nothing had yet occurred to alarm them, and everything promised a successful termination to the journey, when the elephant, after a few premonitory signs of anxiety, halted.

It was four o'clock p.m.

" What is the matter?" asked Sir Francis Cromarty as he looked over the top of the howdah.

" I do not know, sir," said the guide, who was listening to a curious murmuring sound which came confusedly through the thick wood.

Before long the noise became more distinct. It was something like a mingling of human voices and musical instruments together.

Passepartout was all attention. Mr. Fogg waited patiently and in silence.

The Parsee leaped down, and fastening the elephant to a tree crept into the underwood. In a few minutes he returned and said:

" A procession of Brahmins is coming this way. We must hide if possible."

The guide immediately led the elephant into a thicket without letting the travellers dismount. He was ready to resume his place if flight became necessary, but he thought the thick foliage would conceal them effectually from the passers-by.

The discordant noise of human voices and brass instruments came nearer. A monotonous chant mingled with the drums and cymbals. The head of the procession soon came in sight about fifty paces away, and those who composed it were easily distinguished.

In front came the priests wearing mitres and clad in long lace-trimmed robes; surrounding them was a crowd of men, women, and children singing a funeral psalm accompanied by the instruments at intervals. Behind these, on a large car, the wheels of which were ornamented with figures of serpents, came a hideous goddess drawn by four richly-caparisoned Zebus. This idol had four arms; the body was painted a dull red colour, the eyes were staring, the hair was matted, the tongue was hanging out between lips stained with henna and betel. Round the neck of the image was a necklace of skulls; it was girt with a belt of human hands; it was supported upright on the headless trunk of some enormous figure.

Sir Francis Cromarty recognized this idol.

" It is the goddess Kâli," he whispered, " the goddess of love and death."

" I can understand it being the goddess of death, but not of love," replied Passepartout. " What a disgusting hag it is!"

The Parsee made signs to him to hold his tongue.

59

Around the statue a number of fakirs were dancing. These men were stained with ochre and covered with wounds, from which the blood was dripping. These were the sort of idiots who would throw themselves under the Juggernaut car.

Behind them came some Brahmins, clad with Oriental magnificence. They were dragging a woman between them who could hardly sustain herself.

This woman was young and as fair as a European. Her head, neck, shoulders, ears, arms, hands, and ankles were bedecked with jewels or bangles and rings. Her gold lace tunic, over which she wore a thin robe of muslin, revealed the contour of her figure.

Immediately behind, and in terrible contrast to this young woman, came a guard, armed with naked sabres and pistols, carrying a corpse in a palanquin.

It was the dead body of an old man, clothed in the rich dress of a rajah. He wore, as when alive, the pearl-embroidered turban, a silk robe ornamented with gold, a cashmere girdle, studded with diamonds, and the magnificent weapons of an Indian prince.

The procession was closed by a body-guard of fanatics, whose cries drowned even the brass instruments.

Sir Francis Cromarty watched the procession with a peculiarly sad expression, and, turning to the Parsee, said:

"It is a suttee."

The man nodded and put his finger to his lips. The long procession wound about among the trees and disappeared in the depths of the forest.

By degrees the singing died away, and soon the tumult was succeeded by profound silence.

Phileas Fogg had heard what Sir Francis had said, and as soon as the procession had disappeared he asked what a suttee was.

"A suttee," replied the general, "is a human sacrifice, but a voluntary one. That woman you saw will be burnt to-morrow at daybreak."

"The brutes!" exclaimed Passepartout involuntarily.

"And that dead body?" said Mr. Fogg.

"That is the prince, her husband," replied the guide. "He was an independent rajah of Bundelcund."

"What!" said Fogg, without the least emotion, however, "do the English permit these sacrifices?"

"They are not allowed over the greater part of India," replied Sir Francis, "but we have no influence in these barbarous districts. All the territory on the northern slope of the Vindhias is the theatre of murder and pillage."

"Poor woman!" murmured Passepartout, "to be burned alive!"

"Yes," continued the general, "and if she were not burned her existence would be torture. Her relations would shave off her hair, feed her very rarely, and only on rice; they would look upon her as an unclean animal, and she would die like a dog. The prospect of such inhuman treatment, even more than religious fanaticism or affection for the dead, compels the widows to submit to the sacrifice. But occasionally the act is really voluntary, and the energetic interference of Government is necessary. Not long ago, when I was in Bombay, a young widow asked permission to be burnt with her husband's body. The governor, as you may imagine, refused the request. The widow then left the town, took refuge with an independent rajah, and burnt herself to her satisfaction."

The Parsee guide nodded assent to the truth of this anecdote, and said:

"But the suttee to-morrow will not be voluntary."

" How do you know?"

" Everybody in Bundelcund knows that," replied the guide.

" But the woman offered no resistance," said Sir Francis.

" Because she was drugged with the fumes of opium and hemp."

" Where are they taking her to now?"

" To the pagoda of Pillaji, two miles from here. There she will await the time appointed for the sacrifice."

" And that will be——?"

" To-morrow at daybreak."

As he spoke the guide led the elephant out of the thicket and climbed on to the neck of the animal, but just as he was about to urge it to proceed Mr. Fogg stopped him and said to Sir Francis Cromarty:

" Suppose we were to save this woman?"

" Save the woman, Mr. Fogg!" exclaimed the general.

" I have still twelve hours to spare. I can devote them to this adventure."

" Well, I believe you have a heart after all," said Sir Francis Cromarty.

" Occasionally," replied Mr. Fogg, " when I have time."

CHAPTER XIII

In which Passepartout proves once again that fortune favours the brave

The project was a brave one, surrounded with difficulties, and almost impracticable. Mr. Fogg was about to risk his life, or at least his liberty, and consequently the success of his expedition. But he did not hesitate, and he found in Sir Francis Cromarty a ready ally.

Passepartout was entirely at their service. He had

a higher opinion of his master than ever. He began to love Phileas Fogg, who, he perceived, had a heart after all under his cold exterior.

But what part would the guide take in this affair ? He might side with the Hindoos. But if he would not assist, they felt they must keep him neutral.

Sir Francis Cromarty put the question to him frankly.

" I am a Parsee," replied the guide. " The woman is a Parsee also. I am at your disposal."

" Very good," replied Mr. Fogg.

" There is one thing you must recollect," replied the Parsee, " that not only do we risk our lives, but we shall be horribly tortured if we are caught. So take care."

" That is understood," replied Mr. Fogg; " but we had better wait until nightfall before we do anything."

" I think so too," replied the guide.

The Parsee then gave his employers some details respecting the intended victim. She was a celebrated Parsee beauty, the daughter of one of the richest merchants of Bombay. She had been educated on English principles, and her manners accordingly were almost European. Her name was Aouda.

An orphan, she had been married against her will to this old Rajah of Bundelcund, and in three months she was a widow. Knowing the fate that awaited her she escaped, but was recaptured, and the rajah's relations, who were interested in her death, had devoted her to the suttee.

This information only confirmed Mr. Fogg and his friends in their generous resolution. It was decided that the guide should take them as near the pagoda as was consistent with safety.

Half-an-hour afterwards they halted in the brushwood, about five hundred paces from the pagoda, and though they could not see it, they could hear the cries of the Hindoos.

The means by which the victim should be released were then discussed. The guide knew the pagoda very well. Was it possible, did he think, to enter while all the priests were wrapped in their drunken sleep, or could they get in by boring a hole in the wall?

That is a question which can only be decided on the spot, but it was quite certain that whatever they did must be done at night, and not when the victim was being led to the sacrifice, for then nothing could save her.

So they waited. It would be dark about six o'clock, and then they could make a reconnaissance. By that time the Hindoos would be thoroughly intoxicated with "bhang," which is liquid opium mixed with hemp, and it might then be possible to enter the temple.

The Parsee led his employers noiselessly through the forest. After advancing for ten minutes they reached a stream, from which, by the light of the burning torches, they could distinguish the funeral pile, which was composed of sandal-wood, and already impregnated with perfumed oil. Upon this was laid the embalmed body of the rajah, which was about to be burned with his widow. About a hundred paces from the funeral pile was the pagoda, the minarets of which rose through the trees surrounding it.

"This way," whispered the guide.

With redoubled caution, and followed closely by his companions, the man glided silently through the tall grass.

Only the murmur of the wind in the trees broke the profound silence.

The guide soon stopped at the extremity of the cleared space, which was lighted by the torches. Groups of tipsy sleepers lay around—men, women, and children all together—and the ground looked as if it had been the scene of a battle, and these were dead bodies. Only a few drunkards staggered about.

In the background rose the temple, but, greatly to the guide's disappointment, a guard of rajahs was keeping watch at the doors, walking up and down with drawn swords. No doubt the priests were equally vigilant inside.

The Parsee did not advance farther. He saw that it was impossible to force an entrance into the temple, and he drew back with his companions, who, seeing that nothing could be done, stopped and consulted together.

"Let us wait," said the general; "it is only eight o'clock, and the guards will go to sleep before morning."

"That is not unlikely," replied the Parsee.

So they laid down under the trees and waited.

The time appeared very long. Now and then the Parsee went out to reconnoitre; the guard was still on the alert, and an uncertain light came through the windows of the pagoda from the inside.

They waited until midnight; there was no change in the situation. It was evident that the guards did not intend to go to sleep; they had not indulged in any intoxicating beverage. It now became necessary for the party to try to cut through the wall to the pagoda; but then there was the chance of finding the priests inside as wide awake as the guards outside.

After a final discussion the guide said he was ready to proceed. The others followed; they made a long detour so as to reach the pagoda at the back.

About half-past twelve they reached the walls without having met anyone. No guard had been stationed at that side, but then there were no doors or windows to guard.

The night was dark. The last quarter of the moon scarcely rose above the horizon, which was concealed by thick clouds. The height of the trees also added to the obscurity.

But it was not sufficient to have reached the walls; they would have to cut through them. To do this Phileas Fogg and his companions had only their pocket-knives. Fortunately the walls of the temple were made of a mixture of brick and wood which was not very difficult to pierce. A brick once removed, the rest would be easy.

They set to work with as little noise as possible. The Parsee on one side, and Passepartout on the other, worked at a section of bricks so as to get an opening of two feet wide.

The work was progressing when a cry was heard from the interior of the temple, and was taken up by others outside.

Passepartout and the others ceased work. Had the alarm been given? At any rate common prudence demanded a retreat, and the party once more retired under cover of the trees to wait till the alarm was over, but quite ready to continue their work.

But unfortunately the guards began to surround the pagoda completely, and all approach was prevented.

It would be difficult to describe the disappointment of the four men. Now how could they possibly succeed in saving the victim? Sir Francis Cromarty clenched his hands. Passepartout was beside himself, and even the guide had some difficulty in controlling his feelings. The impassible Fogg alone made no sign.

" I suppose we must go," said the general.

" I don't think we can do any more," replied the guide.

" Wait," said Fogg; " it will be time enough if I am at Allahabad before midday."

" But what do you expect to do?" said Sir Francis.

" It will soon be daylight, and then——"

" We may get an opportunity at the last minute."

Sir Francis wished he could see Mr. Fogg's face. What was the cool Englishman calculating on? Did he intend to throw himself upon the pile and snatch the woman away openly?

That would have been madness, and Mr. Fogg was not likely to do such a thing. Nevertheless, Sir Francis consented to wait the *dénouement*. Meanwhile the guide would not permit his companions to remain where they were. He led them to another part of the clearing, whence, under the shade of the brushwood, they could see the sleeping groups.

All this time Passepartout had been turning an idea over in his head, and at last it had taken possession of him. He had begun by thinking his project idiotic ; he ended by looking upon it as feasible.

At any rate he had so far made up his mind that he glided, with the subtleness of a serpent, along one of the lower branches of a tree, the extremity of which almost touched the ground.

The time passed slowly, and at length some indications of dawn appeared, but it was still very dark.

This was the time appointed for the sacrifice. The tomtoms sounded, and the sleeping groups arose as if on the resurrection day. The cries and shouts arose anew. The hour had come!

Then the doors of the pagoda were opened, and a strong light flashed out. The spectators could see the victim dragged forth by two priests. It seemed to Mr. Fogg and Sir Francis Cromarty that the instinct of self-preservation had counteracted the effects of the drug, and the unhappy woman was endeavouring to escape. Sir Francis Cromarty was as much excited, and he seized Mr. Fogg's hand convulsively; in it was grasped an open knife.

The crowd now began to move; the young widow

had been again stupefied with hemp fumes. She passed forth amongst the fakirs who accompanied her with religious vociferations.

Phileas Fogg and his companions mingled with the outskirts of the crowd, and followed.

They soon arrived on the bank of the stream and halted within fifty paces of the funeral pile on which the corpse of the rajah was lying. In the uncertain light they could see the victim stretched motionless by the side of the dead body of her spouse.

A torch was applied to the pile, which was quickly in flames.

Sir Francis Cromarty and the guide were obliged to restrain Phileas Fogg, who in his generous rage was rushing towards the blazing mass.

He had just succeeded in repulsing them when the scene changed. A cry of terror rose from the crowd as they fell to the earth.

The old rajah was not dead after all. He was standing upright on the blazing pile, then raising his young wife in his arms he descended from the pyre in the midst of the columns of whirling smoke, which gave him a spectral appearance.

The fakirs, the guards, the priests, seized with a sudden terror, lay prone upon the earth, not daring to behold such a miracle.

The inanimate victim was lying in her husband's vigorous arms. Mr. Fogg and Sir Francis Cromarty were still standing upright. The Parsee had bowed his head and Passepartout was, no doubt, equally stupefied.

The spectre came close to where Mr. Fogg and Sir Francis were standing, and said hurriedly:

" Let us be off."

It was Passepartout himself who had managed to reach the pyre unperceived in the thick smoke, and profiting by the obscurity had snatched the young lady from death. With wonderful audacity he had passed through the midst of the terrified crowd.

In an instant the four men had disappeared in the wood, and the elephant was bearing them away at a rapid trot. But the cries and shouts, and at last a bullet which went through Mr. Fogg's hat, told them the trick had been discovered, for the body of the old rajah still lay upon the burning pile, and the priests, now recovered from their fear, saw that a rescue had been accomplished.

They immediately dashed into the forest, followed by the guards. A volley was fired after the fugitives, but in a few minutes they had escaped, and were out of range of bullets and arrows.

CHAPTER XIV

Phileas Fogg descends the beautiful Valley of the Ganges without looking at the scenery

The bold attempt had succeeded. In an hour after its accomplishment Passepartout was still laughing at his success. Sir Francis Cromarty had shaken him by the hand. His master had said, " Well done, Passepartout," and such commendation from Mr. Fogg was praise indeed. To which the valet had responded that the credit of the whole business belonged to his master. He himself had only conceived a curious idea, and he laughed still more when he thought that he, the former gymnast, the ex-sergeant of the fire brigade, had played the part of husband to such a charming widow of an embalmed rajah.

The lady herself was still insensible; enveloped in a railway-rug she was reclining in one of the howdahs.

All this time the elephant, guided by the Parsee, was

rapidly threading the gloomy forest. In the course of an hour an immense plain was reached. At seven o'clock they halted. The young lady was still prostrate. The guide forced a few drops of brandy down her throat, but she did not even then recover from her stupor.

Sir Francis Cromarty knew that the effects of the drug were not dangerous, so he was not alarmed at her continued insensibility.

But if her present restoration was not a subject of anxiety to Sir Francis Cromarty, he was less assured respecting her life in future. He did not hesitate to tell Phileas Fogg that if Mrs. Aouda remained in India she would inevitably fall into the hands of her executioners. These fanatical people were to be found all over the peninsula, and would surely claim their victim, the English police notwithstanding. In support of this statement Sir Francis cited a similar case which had lately occurred, and he advised that Mrs. Aouda should be taken out of India altogether; then, and only then, would she be safe.

Phileas Fogg replied that he would consider the suggestion.

About ten o'clock the guide informed the party that they were close to Allahabad. There they would be able to make use of the railway, and in less than four-and-twenty hours would reach Calcutta.

Phileas Fogg would in that case have time to catch the steamer for Hong Kong, which would sail upon the 25th of October at noon.

The young lady was meantime made as comfortable as possible in the waiting-room, while Passepartout was dispatched to purchase some necessary articles of female apparel. Mr. Fogg supplied the money to any desired amount.

Passepartout hastened through the streets of the town—the City of God—one of the most sacred in

India, because it is built at the confluence of the Jumna and Ganges, the two holy streams, the waters of which attract pilgrims from all parts of the peninsula. It is said that the Ganges had its source in heaven, and Brahma kindly permits it to flow to earth.

While he made his purchases Passepartout looked about him, but he perceived that commerce no longer takes its place in the city. Vainly did he ask for such shops as he could have easily seen in Regent Street. There was nothing more imposing than the shop of a Jew, an " old-clothesman," a difficult one to deal with. From this person Passepartout purchased a tweed dress, a splendid cloak, and a sealskin jacket, for which he unhesitatingly paid seventy-five pounds sterling. Then he returned to the railway-station in triumph.

By this time Mrs. Aouda had in some degree recovered, and her beautiful eyes were gradually assuming their wonted softness of expression.

The poet-king Uçaf-Uddaul, celebrating the charms of the Queen of Ahmehnagara, says:

" Her shining hair, parted in the centre, set off the harmonious contour of her white and delicate cheeks, bright with health and the freshness of youth. Her dark eyebrows had the curve of the bow of Kama, the god of Love, and under her long lashes her black eyes swim as the heavenly beams are reflected in the holy lakes of the Himalayas. Her beautiful and even teeth shine between her smiling lips as the half open petals of the passion-flower. Her tiny ears of divinely-curving shape, her small hands and little tender feet, are radiant with pearls of Ceylon or diamonds from the mines of Golconda. Her round and supple waist, which may be spanned by one human hand, expands into curving outlines of her hips and a full and swelling bust, wherein youth in full bloom expands its perfect treasures; and under the clinging folds of her dress the limbs are shown cast in apparently a silver mould by the divine Vicvacarma, the immortal sculptor."

But without continuing our poetic quotation, it may be affirmed that Mrs. Aouda was a most charming woman, and in the European acceptation of the term. She spoke English purely, and the guide had not exaggerated when he had said that the Parsee lady had been transformed by her education.

But now the train was about to start. The Parsee was waiting. Mr. Fogg soon paid him the sum agreed upon—not a farthing more or less. This astonished Passepartout, who knew what they owed to their guide's devotion. The Parsee had indeed risked his life voluntarily, and if he should ever be found out the Hindoos would visit his offence very severely.

The elephant still remained to be dealt with. What would Mr. Fogg do with an animal which had cost him so much? He had already made up his mind about Kiouni, however.

"Parsee," said Mr. Fogg, "you have behaved extremely well. I have paid you for your services, but not for your devotedness. Do you wish for the elephant? If so, he is yours."

The eyes of the guide sparkled with delight.

"Your honour is giving me a fortune!" he said.

"Take it," replied Mr. Fogg, "and even then I shall be indebted to you."

"Himah!" exclaimed Passepartout, "take it, my friend. Kiouni is a splendid beast."

As he spoke Passepartout gave the animal a few pieces of sugar, saying:

"Here, Kiouni, take these."

The elephant thanked him with a few grunts. Then seizing Passepartout round the waist, and wrapping his trunk round the astonished valet, he lifted him from the ground. Passepartout, by no means alarmed, continued to pat the animal, which soon put him down gently, and to the pressure of Kiouni's trunk the man replied with a caressing thump.

Soon after the Europeans were comfortably seated in the train, which was speeding towards Benares. The distance from Allahabad to Benares (eighty miles) was accomplished in two hours, and by that time Mrs. Aouda had quite recovered her usual serenity.

What was her astonishment to find herself in the railway-carriage dressed in European garb, and in company with travellers absolutely unknown to her !

Her companions paid her every attention, and the general told her what had occurred. He particularly dwelt upon the devotion of Mr. Fogg, who had risked his life in her cause; and he extolled Passepartout's courage also.

Mr. Fogg said nothing to all this, and Passepartout kept saying that he had done nothing remarkable at all.

Mrs. Aouda thanked her deliverers by tears as well as by words. Her lovely eyes expressed her gratitude. Then as the thought of the suttee occurred to her, and when she perceived that she was still on Indian territory, she shuddered with fear.

Phileas Fogg quite understood what was passing in her mind, and hastened to reassure her by offering to take her to Hong Kong till the affair had blown over.

Mrs. Aouda accepted this offer gratefully, for at Hong Kong a relative of hers was living. He was one of the principal merchants of the place, which is so absolutely English though in China.

At half-past twelve the train reached Benares. The Brahmic legends state that the town is built upon the site of the ancient Casi, which was formerly suspended in space, like Mahomet's coffin. But in this practical

73

age Benares rests upon *terra firma*, and Passepartout saw many brick-built houses amongst the native huts of clay.

Here Sir Francis Cromarty quitted the train. The troops of which he was in command were encamped in the northern part of the town. The brigadier took leave of Phileas Fogg, wishing him every success, and expressing a hope that he would continue his journey in a more profitable and less eccentric manner. Mrs. Aouda's adieux were almost affectionate in their warmth. She could never forget how much she was indebted to Sir Francis Cromarty. As for Passepartout, he was honoured with another warm clasp of the hand, and was much moved by the general's condescension. Then the party separated.

Leaving Benares, the railroad traverses the valley of the Ganges. The scenery was varied; the hills were covered with verdure, and the fields were rich in corn. The jungles were full of alligators, the villages were neatly built, and the forests were very thick. Elephants were bathing themselves in the sacred Ganges, as well as bands of Hindoos of both sexes, who notwithstanding the lateness of the season, were performing their pious ablutions. These faithful ones were deadly enemies of Buddhism, and were strict Brahmins, who believed in Vishnu, the Sun God; Siva, the embodiment of natural forces; and Brahma, the chief of priests and lawgivers. But how these three gentlemen regard India, now thoroughly "Anglicized," with steamers cutting through the sacred waters of the Ganges, and frightening the animals upon the banks, we cannot say!

The landscape skimmed past, and was occasionally hidden altogether by steam from the engine. The fort of Chunar was noticed, then came Ghazepore and its famous rose-water factories. Lord Cornwallis's tomb was sighted on the left bank, and the fortified town of Buxar. Patna, the great commercial city, and the principal opium market in India, and Monghir, a town as English as Manchester or Birmingham with its tall factory chimneys vomiting black smoke.

Night fell, and in the midst of the roarings of tigers, the growling and snarling of bears and wolves, the train passed on at full speed, and none of the marvels of Bengal were perceived—Golconda, Gour, now in ruins, Mourshedabad, the former capital, Houghly, Chandernagor, in French territory, where Passepartout would have been proud to have seen his country's flag, were all successively passed.

They reached Calcutta at length at seven a.m. The Hong Kong steamer was not to start till noon, so Mr. Fogg had five hours to spare.

According to his reckoning he was due at Calcutta on the 15th of October, twenty-three days after leaving London and here he was at Calcutta at the prescribed time. Unfortunately the two days gained between London and Bombay had been lost, as we know, while crossing the peninsula. But we must not imagine that Phileas Fogg regretted what he had done—no, not for a moment.

CHAPTER XV

The bag of notes is lightened by several thousand pounds more !

When the train entered the station Passepartout was the first to alight. Mr. Fogg had counted upon proceeding at once to the steamer and disposing Mrs. Aouda comfortably therein, as he was unwilling to leave her so long as she was upon Indian territory.

Just as Mr. Fogg was leaving the station a policeman approached and said:

" Mr. Phileas Fogg, I believe?"

" Yes."

" Is this your servant?" the policeman continued, indicating Passepartout.

" Yes."

" Will you have the kindness to follow me?"

Mr. Fogg did not permit a word to escape him, nor did he make any movement of surprise. This man represented the law, and to all Englishmen the law is a sacred thing. Passepartout, like a Frenchman as he was, wanted to argue the point, but the policeman touched him with his staff, and Phileas Fogg made a sign to him to obey.

" This young lady can accompany us I presume?" said Phileas Fogg.

" She can, certainly," replied the policeman, who then led the way to a " palki-ghari," a four-wheeled vehicle, carrying four people, and drawn by two horses. They drove away, and nobody said a word till the carriage stopped again.

The carriage traversed the Black Town with its narrow streets and cosmopolitan population, and then went through the European quarter, the brick houses, handsome equipages, and well-dressed people making quite a gay appearance even at that early hour.

The palki-ghari stopped before a quiet-looking house, and the policeman told his prisoners, as we may call them, to alight; he then conducted them to a room with barred windows, and said:

" At half-past eight you will be brought before Judge Obadiah."

He then went out and locked the door.

" So we are prisoners!" exclaimed Passepartout as he threw himself into a chair.

Mrs. Aouda meantime begged Mr. Fogg, with tears, to leave her to her fate. " It is on my account that you have been pursued, it is for having saved me that you are arrested."

Phileas Fogg quietly replied that such a thing was impossible. The complainants in the suttee case would not dare to appear. It was a mistake, and Mr. Fogg said that in any case he was determined to conduct Mrs. Aouda to Hong Kong.

" But the boat starts at noon," observed Passepartout.

" We shall be on board before that," replied Mr. Fogg.

This was said so confidently that Passepartout muttered, " Oh! then it will be all right," but in his innermost soul he was not so sure of it.

At half-past eight the policeman entered and ushered the prisoners into the next room. This was the court, and was already well filled with a miscellaneous audience.

The prisoners were accommodated on a bench opposite the desk of the judge, who almost immediately entered, followed by his clerk. Judge Obadiah was a fat round-faced man; he took down a wig from a nail and put it on his head.

" Call the first case," he said.

But immediately putting his hand to his head, he exclaimed, " This is not my wig!"

" No, your honour, it is mine," replied the clerk.

" My dear Mr. Oyster Puff, how can you fancy a judge can give proper decisions if he wears a clerk's wig?"

The exchange of wigs was effected. During this dialogue Passepartout had been burning with impatience, while the hands of the clock were fast advancing towards noon.

" Call the first case," repeated the judge.

" Phileas Fogg," said the clerk.

" Here I am."

" Passepartout."

" Present."

" Good," said the judge; " we have been waiting for you for two days, and have examined all the trains from Bombay."

" But of what are we accused?" asked Passepartout impatiently.

" You will know in good time," replied the judge.

" Sir," said Mr. Fogg, " I am a British subject, and by rights——"

" Have you been badly treated?" asked Mr. Obadiah.

" By no means, but——"

" Very well then, call the complainants."

As the judge spoke the door opened, and three Hindoo priests were ushered in.

" Oh! that is it," muttered Passepartout; " those are the scoundrels who wanted to burn our young lady."

The priests stood up before the judge, and the clerk read the accusation of sacrilege against Phileas Fogg and his servant, who had defiled a temple of the Brahmins.

" You have heard the charge?" said the judge to Phileas Fogg.

" Yes," he replied, looking at his watch, " and I admit it."

" You admit it?"

" Yes, and I want to hear what these priests will in their turn confess concerning their doings at the Pillaji."

The priests looked at each other. They evidently did not understand to what Fogg referred.

" Of course," exclaimed Passepartout impetuously —" at the pagoda where they were going to burn their victim."

The priests were more astonished than ever, and Judge Obadiah was almost equally so.

"What victim?" he asked. "To burn whom? In the town of Bombay?"

"Bombay?" exclaimed Passepartout.

"Of course; it is not the pagoda of Pillaji, but the pagoda of Malabar Hill at Bombay, we are referring to."

"And as a proof," said the clerk, "here are the shoes of the profaner of the temple."

As he spoke he placed a pair of shoes before him on the desk.

"My shoes!" cried Passepartout, who could not restrain this incautious declaration.

The confusion may be imagined. The incident of the Bombay pagoda had been forgotten by the travellers, but it was for this offence that they were brought before the Calcutta magistrates.

Fix had seen the great advantage he could obtain, so he delayed his departure from Bombay for twelve hours. He consulted with the priests, and promised them compensation, as he knew very well that the English Government would severely punish any crime of this nature. He had sent the priests on by train, and owing to the time spent by Fogg and his party in releasing Aouda, Fix and the priests reached Calcutta first, though in any case Fogg and his servant would have been arrested in Calcutta in consequence of a telegram from the authorities in Bombay. Fix was much disappointed to find that Fogg had not reached Calcutta. He thought that the eccentric gentleman must have stopped at some intermediate station and taken refuge in the southern provinces. For twenty-four hours Fix had restlessly paced the Calcutta station, and his joy can be imagined when he that morning perceived the party descending from the train, though he could not account for the presence of the lady. He at once told a policeman to arrest Mr. Fogg and that is how they all came before Judge Obadiah.

If Passepartout had been less occupied he would have perceived the detective in a corner of the justice-room watching the proceedings with an interest easy to be understood; for at Calcutta, as at Bombay and Suez, he still waited for the warrant of arrest.

However, Judge Obadiah had noticed Passepartout's confession, which the valet would gladly have ignored.

" The facts are admitted, then?" said the judge.

" Yes," replied Mr. Fogg.

" Well," continued the judge, " as the English law is intended to protect all religions equally, and as the man Passepartout has confessed his crime, and is convicted of having violated the sanctity of the pagoda at Malabar Hill, in Bombay, on the 20th of October, the said Passepartout is condemned to fifteen days' imprisonment and a fine of three hundred pounds sterling."

" Three hundred pounds!" exclaimed Passepartout, who was conscious only of that portion of the sentence.

" Silence!" cried the usher.

" And," continued the judge, " as it has not been proved that the master aided and abetted the sacrilege, but as he must be held responsible for his servant's acts, the said Phileas Fogg is sentenced to eight days' imprisonment and to a fine of one hundred and fifty pounds. Usher, call the next case."

Fix, in his corner, rubbed his hands with delight. Phileas Fogg was detained eight days in Calcutta; that would give time for the warrant to arrive from England. Passepartout was completely upset; his condemnation would ruin his master, whose bet of twenty thousand pounds would be lost, and all because he, Passepartout, had gone like an idiot into that cursed pagoda.

But Phileas Fogg did not appear in the least concerned. As the usher was calling the next case Fogg rose and said:

" I offer bail."

" You can do so," said the judge.

Fix's blood ran cold, but he recovered himself when he heard the judge say that as Fogg and his servant were strangers, a bail of a thousand pounds each would be necessary.

That was two thousand pounds Mr. Fogg would have to pay if he did not appear.

" I will pay," said that gentleman, and from the bag which Passepartout carried he drew a roll of banknotes and placed them on the clerk's desk.

" The money will be repaid when you come out of prison," said the judge; " meantime you are free on bail."

" Come," said Fogg to his servant.

" But at least they ought to give me my shoes," said Passepartout in a rage.

They gave him back his shoes.

" They have cost us dear," he muttered; " more than a thousand pounds each, without counting the inconvenience."

Passepartout slunk out after Mr. Fogg, who had given his arm to the young lady. Fix still hoped that the robber would not abandon such a large sum as two thousand pounds, and that he would eventually go to prison, so he hurried after the party.

Mr. Fogg took a carriage, in which he, Mrs. Aouda, and Passepartout were driven to the quays.

The *Rangoon* was moored half a mile out. The blue-peter was flying at the fore. It was eleven o'clock, and there was still an hour to spare. Fix saw the three travellers take a boat and go out to the ship. The detective stamped his foot.

"The rascal!" he cried. "So he is going. Two thousand pounds sacrifice! He is as reckless as a robber; but I will follow him to the end of the world if necessary, but at this rate the money will soon be expended."

The detective had some reason for his remark, for what with expenses and "tips," the purchase of the elephant, fines and bail, Phileas Fogg had actually expended five thousand pounds since he had left London, and this was diminishing considerably the sum of money the detective hoped to recover.

CHAPTER XVI

Fix does not appear to understand all that is said to him

The *Rangoon*, one of the P. & O. Company's steamers on the China and Japan line, was an iron screw ship of about 1,770 tons burden, with engines of 400 horse-power. She was as fast as the *Mongolia* but not so comfortable; and Mrs. Aouda was not so comfortable as Fogg wished. But after all, the voyage was only three thousand five hundred miles long—that is, eleven or twelve days' steaming—and the young lady was not difficult to please.

Mrs. Aouda became well acquainted with Phileas Fogg in a few days, and lost no opportunity of expressing her gratitude to him. That phlegmatic gentleman listened with the greatest coolness, and showed no emotion whatever. He took care, however, that the lady should want for nothing, and passed hours with her every day, if not talking, at least listening to her conversation. He was most polite, but his politeness was somewhat automatic. Mrs. Aouda did not know what to think, but Passepartout had informed her how eccentric his master was, and told her of his wager to go round the world. Mrs. Aouda laughed at this, but after all she owed him her life, and her rescuer would not lose by being viewed through a halo of romance.

Mrs. Aouda confirmed the Hindoo guide's report respecting herself. She was of the highest native caste. Many Parsee merchants have made great fortunes in India. One of them, Sir Jamsetjee Jejeebhoy, has been made a baronet by the Queen, and Mrs. Aouda was connected with his family. It was a cousin of his whom she expected to meet at Hong Kong, and hoped that he would afford her protection and assistance, but at any rate Mr. Fogg bade her not worry herself, for everything would come all right. His actual words were, " It will be all square."

The young lady scarcely understood him; she fixed her liquid eyes upon him, but the unimpressible Fogg was as stiff as ever, and made no response.

The first portion of the voyage was very favourable ; the weather was fine, and everything went well. The *Rangoon* soon sighted the Great Andaman, the chief of that group of islands, with its picturesque mountain called Saddle Peak, a landmark to all sailors, as it is two thousand four hundred feet high.

The *Rangoon* proceeded along the coast, but they saw none of the savage natives. The appearance of the islands was superb; immense forests of palm, teak, and mimosas covered the foreground, and at the back the hills rose against the clear sky. In the cliffs were thousands of swallows, the nests of which are so eagerly sought as food in China. But the *Rangoon* rapidly steamed past the Andamans towards the straits of Malacca, which give access to the China Sea.

But what was Fix—who had been dragged against his will in this trip round the world—doing all this

83

time? Before he left Calcutta he had given instructions that the warrant for Mr. Fogg's arrest should be sent to him at *Hong Kong*, and he had then embarked on board the *Rangoon* unperceived by Passepartout, and hoped to remain unrecognized during the voyage; in fact, it would have been difficult to account for his presence on board without arousing the suspicions of Passepartout, who believed him to be in Bombay. But it was fated that he should meet the valet, as we shall see.

All Fix's hopes were now centred in Hong Kong, for the steamer would not stop long enough at Singapore to enable him to do anything there; the arrest must be made at Hong Kong or not at all.

Hong Kong is English territory, but it was the last that they would meet on their voyage round the world. Beyond it, China, Japan, and America would offer Mr. Fogg a safe refuge. So if the warrant were found at Hong Kong, Fogg could be arrested and handed over to the local police, but after that a writ of extradition would be necessary for his arrest, and this would give rise to all kinds of difficulties of which the man might take advantage and finally escape. If Fix did not settle the matter at Hong Kong he had no chance of success.

" Now," Fix would say to himself, as he sat for hours in his cabin—" now either the warrant will be at Hong Kong and I shall arrest the fellow, or it will not be there. In the latter case I must delay his departure at all hazards. I have failed hitherto, and if I lose him now my reputation will be gone; but how am I to stop him? That is the question."

As a last resource, then, Fix made up his mind to tell Passepartout everything, and let him know what sort of a man he served, for the valet was evidently not an accomplice. Under the circumstances Passepartout would no doubt assist; but it was a dangerous game to play, and should only be tried when all other means failed. A hint given by Passepartout to Mr. Fogg would cause a final failure.

The detective was therefore in a fix, and Mrs. Aouda's presence on board with Mr. Fogg embarrassed him still more.

Who was this woman? and what circumstances had made her Fogg's companion? They must have met between Bombay and Calcutta; but where? Was it by chance, or had he expected to meet this charming person?—for that she was charming Fix had already seen in the court-house.

He was puzzled to think whether there had been an elopement, and at last he made up his mind there had been; but if so, what advantage could he gain from it? Whether she was married or not the fact of the elopement remained, and his knowledge of this might so work upon Mr. Fogg that he would not be able to leave Hong Kong without paying him a heavy sum of money.

But it was first necessary to get to Hong Kong, and Fogg had a very unpleasant habit of jumping from one steamer to another, and so before anything was settled he might be off again. The thing to do evidently was to telegraph the approach of the *Rangoon* from Singapore.

In any case, however, he determined to question Passepartout first. He knew it was not difficult to make the lad talk, and Fix decided to make himself known. There was no time to lose; the steamer was due at Singapore next day. So Fix left his cabin, and seeing Passepartout on deck the detective rushed towards him with every appearance of surprise, exclaiming:

" What! are *you* on board?"

"Mr. Fix," replied Passepartout, who was much astonished to recognize his travelling companion on board the *Mongolia*; "Why I left you at Bombay, and I find you on the way to Hong Kong! Are you also going round the world?"

"Oh no," replied Fix, "I am going to stop at Hong Kong a few days—that is——"

"Oh!" said Passepartout; "but how is it I have not seen you on board before to-day?"

"The fact is I have been rather sea-sick, and obliged to keep below; the Bay of Bengal does not agree with me as well as the Indian Ocean. Well, how is your master, Mr. Fogg?"

"Oh, perfectly well, and keeping his time regularly. He is not a day late. Ah, Mr. Fix, we have got a young lady with us now."

"A young lady!" exclaimed the detective in pretended astonishment.

Passepartout then proceeded to tell Fix all the circumstances connected with Mrs. Aouda's release, the suttee, their escape, the judgment of the Calcutta court, and their release on bail. Fix, who knew all the last part of the story, pretended to ignore the whole of it, and Passepartout was delighted to have such an attentive listener.

"But," said Fix at last, "does your master intend to take this young lady to Europe with him?"

"No, Mr. Fix, by no means. We shall leave her at Hong Kong under the care of a relative, a rich merchant there."

"There is nothing to be done on that score," muttered the detective as he concealed his disappointment. "Come and let us have a glass together, Monsieur Passepartout."

"Willingly, Mr. Fix; the least we can do is to drink to our pleasant meeting on board the *Rangoon*."

CHAPTER XVII

What happened between Singapore and Hong Kong

Passepartout and the detective met frequently after that, but the latter was very reserved, and did not attempt to make Passepartout speak about his master. Once or twice only Fix encountered Mr. Fogg, who kept in his cabin, either attending to Mrs. Aouda or playing his invariable game of whist.

Passepartout, on his part, began to think very seriously of the curious chance that had brought Fix upon his master's track once again. How did it happen that this complacent gentleman, whom they first met at Suez when he embarked on the *Mongolia* and landed at Bombay, where he said he wished to remain, was at that moment on board the *Rangoon* bound for Hong Kong—in a word, following Mr. Fogg? This puzzled Passepartout particularly—it certainly was extraordinary, and what could Fix want? The valet was ready to wager his famous slippers that this man would leave Hong Kong at the same time they did, and probably in the same steamer.

But if Passepartout had puzzled himself for a century he never would have hit upon the true reason. It would not have entered his head that his master was suspected of robbery, and was being traced as a thief, but as it is in human nature to give some explanation of everything, Passepartout finally made up his mind that Fix had been sent out by the members of the Reform Club to see that the conditions of the wager were duly observed.

" I see it all now," said the honest fellow, who was delighted with his own cleverness; " he is a spy sent out by those gentlemen, though I don't think it is a very gentlemanly thing to do, Mr. Fogg is so straightforward and honourable. Your spy, gentlemen, shall cost you dear."

Passepartout, delighted with his discovery, nevertheless determined to say nothing about it to Mr. Fogg for fear of annoying him, but he made up his mind to quiz Fix at every opportunity without betraying himself.

On Wednesday, the 3oth of October, the *Rangoon* entered the Straits of Malacca, and the next day at four o'clock anchored at Singapore to coal.

Phileas Fogg, having noted the gain in his book, this time went ashore, accompanied by Mrs. Aouda, who had expressed a wish to land.

Fix, who was suspicious of Fogg's every movement, followed unperceived, and Passepartout, who was secretly delighted, went about his ordinary avocations.

The island of Singapore is neither large nor imposing; the mountains are wanting, but it is, nevertheless, charming in its own way. It is a park traversed by pretty roads. A good carriage, well horsed, took Mrs. Aouda and Phileas Fogg through palm groves and plantations, where the plants perfumed the air, though the woods were by no means free from tigers, and numerous monkeys gambolled in the trees. If anyone is astonished to hear that tigers are not exterminated in such a small island, they may be told that they swim over from the mainland.

After two hours Mr. Fogg and his companion, still followed by the detective, returned to the ship at ten o'clock, Mr. Fix having been put to the expense of a carriage also.

Passepartout received them on deck. He had purchased a quantity of immense mangoes, which are an extremely agreeable fruit. He offered them to Mrs. Aouda, who received them very gracefully.

At eleven o'clock the *Rangoon* started again, and in a few hours Malacca was out of sight.

88

Thirteen hundred miles now separated them from Hong Kong, and Fogg hoped to get there in six days, so as to leave by steamer for Yokohama on the 6th of November.

The *Rangoon* was very full, for a great many second-class passengers had embarked at the various ports *en route*.

The weather, which had been very fine, now began to change with the waning moon; there was a high sea and a stiff breeze, which, however, was in the south-east, and favourable. The captain hoisted sails whenever he could, and under these circumstances the steamer made great headway, but in the very rough weather the steam was reduced, and the passengers suffered considerably from sea-sickness. The delay did not affect Phileas Fogg apparently, but Passepartout was extremely irritable. He found fault with the captain, the engineer, and the company, and consigned all the Peninsular and Oriental officials to the devil. Perhaps he was thinking of the gas he had left burning in Savile Row, and that may have increased his impatience.

" Are you in such a hurry to get to Hong Kong?" asked the detective one day.

" In a very great hurry," replied Passepartout.

" You think that Mr. Fogg is anxious to catch the Yokohama steamer?"

" I know he is."

" You are a believer, then, in this voyage round the world?"

" Absolutely—and you?"

" I? I don't believe a word of it."

" You are a sly fox," replied Passepartout, winking at him.

This remark rather disconcerted Fix. Was it possible the Frenchman had found him out? He did not know what to do, but how could Passepartout have found him out? And yet he must have had some reason to speak as he did.

On the next occasion the lad spoke still more plainly, and said:

" Are we to lose the pleasure of your society at Hong Kong, Mr. Fix?"

" Well," replied the detective in an embarrassed manner, " I don't know; perhaps——"

" Ah!" said Passepartout, " if you come with us it will be all the better for me; besides, an agent of the P. & O. Company cannot stop half-way. You did not intend to go beyond Bombay, you know, and here you are in China. America is not far off, and thence to Europe is but a step."

Fix looked attentively at his companion, whose face was perfectly innocent, and laughed too. But the valet was in the humour for quizzing, and asked him how much he expected to make out of his present business.

" Oh! I don't get much," replied Fix, " I have good and bad times, but you understand that I do not travel at my own expense."

" Oh! I am quite sure of that," replied Passepartout, laughing louder than ever.

After this Fix returned to his cabin to think over matters. Somehow or other the Frenchman had found him out, but had he told his master? What game was he playing all this time? was the servant an accomplice or not? was the whole business at an end? The detective passed many hours endeavouring to unravel the thread, but he did not know what to do.

However, he at length determined to deal frankly with Passepartout. If he could not find an excuse to arrest Fogg at Hong Kong, and if he was determined to quit English territory, Fix made up his mind to confide in the servant. Either Passepartout was an accomplice and knew everything, or he knew nothing. In the former case Fix knew he would fail; in the latter he thought it would be to the lad's interest to leave his master's service.

Such was the situation; and Fogg appeared to be perfectly indifferent all through. He pursued his course round the world without troubling himself about anything.

But there was danger not far off which might produce certain palpitations of the heart; but, to Passepartout's great surprise, Mrs. Aouda's charms had no effect upon his master.

Yes, it certainly was astonishing to Passepartout, who could read the lady's gratitude towards his master in her eyes. Decidedly Phileas Fogg was wanting in heart. There was no doubt he was brave, but he was not affectionate. There was no evidence or trace that the incidents of the journey had altered his feelings, but Passepartout was continually sunk in reverie. One day he was leaning over the rail looking into the engine-room at the machinery when a sudden lurch of the vessel raised the screw out of the water. The steam escaped roaring by the valves, and provoked an explosion of anger from the worthy Frenchman.

" Those valves are not sufficiently charged. We are making no headway. That is just like the English. Ah, if this were only a Yankee ship! We might, perhaps, blow up eventually, but we should go all the quicker meanwhile."

CHAPTER XVIII

In which Phileas Fogg, Passepartout, and Fix go about their own business respectively

During the last part of the voyage the weather was very tempestuous. A strong north-east wind retarded the progress of the vessel, the *Rangoon* rolled very much, and the passengers suffered in proportion.

During the 3rd and 4th of November the wind rose to a gale, and the vessel was hove to. The captain was of opinion that they would be twenty hours late at Hong Kong if the storm did not abate.

Phileas Fogg watched the furious sea, which appeared determined to thwart his plans, with the greatest coolness. He showed no irritation, although, if the vessel were twenty hours behind time, he would lose the steamer for Yokohama. But it appeared almost as if the tempest were a part of his programme. Mrs. Aouda, who spoke to him on the subject, found him as calm as ever.

Fix, however, did not look upon things in the same light; quite the contrary; but at the same time he was glad the storm had occurred, and would have been more pleased if the *Rangoon* had been obliged to scud before the wind. All this delay was in his favour, for Mr. Fogg would be obliged to remain for some days at Hong Kong. He did not mind being sick, and though his body suffered, in spirit he was delighted.

But Passepartout was extremely angry all this bad weather. They had been all right up till now. Land and water had appeared to be at his master's service. Steamers and railways obeyed him; wind and steam had united in their favour. Had the hour of misfortune arrived? Passepartout felt as if the bet must be paid by himself. This tempest exasperated him, storm made him furious, and he would like to have whipped the sea, poor fellow. Fix had hidden his satisfaction, and well it was he did so, for if Passepartout had divined his secret, Fix would have passed a very bad quarter of an hour.

Passepartout remained on deck during the storm; indeed, it was impossible for him to have remained below; he assisted the crew, and astonished them by his agility. Time after time he interrogated the captain, the officers, and the sailors, but they could not help laughing at him when he wanted to know how long the tempest would last; they only referred him to the barometer, which had not made up its mind to rise. Passepartout shook it, but his blows had no effect upon the stubborn instrument.

At length the tempest subsided. On the 4th of November the sea went down and the wind veered to the southward, which was in their favour.

Passepartout improved with the weather, sails were once more set, and the *Rangoon* proceeded at a very great pace.

But they could not regain the lost time. It could not be helped, and land was not signalled until five a.m. on the 6th of November. Phileas Fogg should have arrived on the 5th, so he was twenty-four hours late, and the Yokohama steamer would therefore be missed.

At six o'clock the pilot came on board to navigate the ship into the harbour of Hong Kong.

Passepartout was dying to ask him whether the Yokohama steamer had started, but he did not dare; he confided his anxiety to Fix, who, sly fox as he was, endeavoured to console him by telling him that Mr. Fogg would be in plenty of time if he took the following steamer. This remark made Passepartout very angry.

But if Passepartout was afraid, Mr. Fogg, having consulted his *Bradshaw*, was not, and he asked the pilot quietly when the Yokohama steamer would leave.

" At to-morrow morning's flood," replied the pilot.

" Ah!" said Mr. Fogg with apparent unconcern.

Passepartout, who was near, would willingly have

embraced the pilot, while Fix would have wrung his neck with equal pleasure.

"What is the vessel's name?" asked Mr. Fogg.

"The *Carnatic*," replied the pilot.

"Ought she not to have sailed yesterday?"

"Yes, sir, but her boilers were out of repair, and her departure was postponed."

"Thank you," replied Mr. Fogg, and he then quietly walked down to the saloon.

Passepartout shook the pilot warmly by the hand, and called him a right down good fellow.

The pilot had not the slightest idea what Passepartout meant by this friendliness; he merely returned whistling to his station on the bridge, and navigated the vessel through a cloud of junks and fishing boats and other vessels in the bay.

At one o'clock the *Rangoon* was alongside the quay, and the passengers landed.

It must be confessed that Phileas Fogg was singularly lucky. But for this accident to her boiler the *Carnatic* would have sailed the day before, in which case the passengers bound for Japan would have been obliged to wait eight days for the next steamer. It is true Mr. Fogg was twenty-four hours late, but this delay was not serious.

In fact, the steamer from Yokohama to San Francisco was in correspondence with the Hong Kong steamer, and would not start before the latter arrived, so the twenty-four hours might easily be made up during the twenty-two days' voyage across the Pacific. As things were, however, Mr. Fogg had lost twenty-four hours in the thirty-five days since he had left London.

The *Carnatic* was not to sail till five o'clock the next morning, so Mr. Fogg had sixteen hours before him. He escorted Mrs. Aouda to the Club House Hotel, where apartments were engaged, and Fogg saw that she wanted for nothing. He then informed her that he was about to seek for her relative; at the same time he gave orders to Passepartout not to leave the hotel till his return.

Mr. Fogg was accordingly conducted to the Exchange, as the most likely place to find the wealthy merchant he sought.

The broker to whom Mr. Fogg addressed himself informed him that the merchant in question had left Hong Kong two years before, and had returned to Europe.

Phileas Fogg immediately returned to the hotel and told Mrs. Aouda the result of his inquiry. She made no reply for a moment, but after reflection she said in a quiet way:

"What ought I to do, Mr. Fogg?"

"It is very simple," he said. "You must return to Europe."

"But I cannot intrude——"

"You do not intrude at all. Passepartout!"

"Sir."

"Go and secure three berths on board the *Carnatic*."

Passepartout, delighted to hear that the young lady was to proceed in their company, immediately obeyed his master's orders.

CHAPTER XIX

Passepartout takes too great an interest in his master.
The result!

Hong Kong is only an island ceded to the English by the treaty of Nankin in 1842. In a few years the colonizing genius of Great Britain had made it a great town and harbour. Hong Kong is situated at the mouth of the Canton River, sixty miles from the Portuguese town of Macao, on the opposite bank. Hong

Kong had vanquished its rival in the commercial struggle, and most of the traffic centres in the English town. There are docks, hospitals, warehouses, a Gothic cathedral, a Government House, macadamized streets, and everything to lead one to suppose that a Kentish town had fallen through to the Antipodes.

Passepartout, with his hands in his pockets, strolled down to Port Victoria, looking about him and admiring all he saw. The town appeared to him very much like any other town colonized by the English.

When he reached Port Victoria he found it swarming with ships of all sorts and of all nations. He also remarked a number of elderly natives clothed in nankeen dress, and on inquiring of the barber where he went to be shaved, the man, who spoke English very well, told him that those old people were all over eighty years of age, and so entitled to wear the imperial colour, yellow. Passepartout thought this rather curious.

Having been shaved he went down to the quay, where the *Carnatic* was lying, and there he perceived Fix walking up and down, looking very much disappointed.

"Good," thought Passepartout. "Things are not going well with the gentlemen of the Reform Club."

He approached the detective smilingly, and without noticing his air of vexation.

Now it was no wonder that Fix was annoyed. The warrant had not arrived, and it was quite possible that it might not reach him for several days. Hong Kong was the last British territory Mr. Fogg would touch upon in his journey, and unless he were detained now all hope of his arrest must be abandoned.

"Well, Mr. Fix, have you made up your mind to come with us to America?" said Passepartout.

"Yes," growled Fix.

96

" Come along, then," said Passepartout, laughing. " I knew you could not get on without us; come and take your berth."

They went to the office and secured four places, but the clerk informed them that the *Carnatic*, being now ready for sea, would sail at eight o'clock that evening instead of next morning, as previously announced.

" All right," replied Passepartout; " that will suit my master. I will go and tell him."

But now Fix made a bold stroke. He determined to tell Passepartout everything. That was his only hope of keeping Fogg in Hong Kong.

As they left the office Fix offered his companion something to drink. Passepartout, having plenty of time, accepted the invitation.

There was a tavern on the quay which looked inviting. This they entered. There was a large decorated room, at the end of which was a cushioned camp bedstead. On this a number of men were reposing.

About thirty people were in the room, seated at small tables. Some were drinking ale or porter, some spirits, and nearly all were smoking long red clay pipes, filled with opium steeped in rose-water. Occasionally a smoker fell under the table, and was at once carried and laid upon the camp bedstead.

Fix and Passepartout immediately perceived that they had entered a smoking-house, frequented by those wretched idiots to whom the English merchants sell opium every year to the value of two hundred and sixty millions of francs—unfortunate creatures as they are, devoted to one of the most injurious of vices.

The Chinese Government has tried to remedy the abuse, but in vain. From the rich the habit of opium-smoking has by degrees descended, and now the drug is used by men and women who, when once accustomed to it, cannot relinquish the habit. A great

A3—G

smoker can consume eight pipefuls in a day, but he dies in five years.

It was to one of these smoking-houses which disgrace Hong Kong that Fix and Passepartout had come for refreshment. The Frenchman had no money, but he accepted the treat in the hope of reciprocating it.

Two bottles of port were ordered, to which Passepartout paid great attention, while Fix watched him narrowly. The travellers talked of many things, chiefly of Fix's determination to sail in the *Carnatic*. This reminded Passepartout that he ought to go and tell Mr. Fogg of the change in the hour of the steamer sailing. As the bottles were empty he rose to do so, but Fix detained him.

" Wait a moment," he said.

" What do you want, Mr. Fix?"

" I want to talk to you seriously."

" Seriously!" exclaimed Passepartout, draining his glass. " Well, then, we can talk to-morrow. I have no time to-day."

" Stay where you are," said Fix. " What I have to say concerns your master."

Passepartout looked at him steadily, and as the detective's expression was peculiar he sat down again.

" What have you to say?" he said.

Fix laid his hand on his companion's arm, and said :

" You have guessed who I am, have you not?"

" I think so," replied Passepartout, smiling.

" Now I am going to confess all."

" Yes, now I know all, my friend, that is not so bad. However, go ahead; but I may tell you that those gentlemen have sent you on a fruitless errand."

" Fruitless!" said Fix. " You evidently do not know the amount in question."

" Yes I do," replied Passepartout; " it is twenty thousand pounds."

"Fifty-five thousand!" replied Fix, shaking his friend's hand.

"What!" exclaimed Passepartout, "Mr. Fogg has risked fifty-five thousand pounds! All the more reason then, that we should not lose any time." He rose as he spoke.

"Fifty-five thousand pounds!" continued Fix, forcing Passepartout to his seat as a flask of brandy was placed on the table, "and if I succeed I shall get two thousand. If you will help me I will give you five hundred."

"Help you!" exclaimed Passepartout in astonishment.

"Yes, help me to keep Mr. Fogg in Hong Kong for a few days."

"What!" said Passepartout, "are you not content with tracking him and suspecting him? Do these gentlemen wish to prevent his further progress? I am ashamed of them."

"What do you mean?" asked Fix.

"I mean that they are mean. They might just as well pick Mr. Fogg's pocket."

"That is just what we want to do."

"Oh, then, it is a conspiracy," exclaimed Passepartout, who, plied with brandy, was getting excited. "And those people call themselves gentlemen and my master's friends!"

Fix was considerably puzzled.

"Friends indeed!" continued Passepartout—"members of the Reform Club, eh? My master is an honest man, Mr. Fix, and when he bets he bets fairly."

"Do you know who I am?" said Fix, looking steadily at Passepartout.

"Yes, you are an agent of the Reform Club, whose business it is to hinder my master's journey, and a mean job it is. I found you out long ago, but I did not like to betray you."

"So he knows nothing about it?" said Fix quickly.

"Nothing whatever," replied Passepartout as he drained his glass once more.

The detective did not know what to do. Passepartout's mistake appeared to be genuine, but this fact rendered his project all the more difficult. The lad was acting in good faith, and was not his master's accomplice as Fix had feared, and he therefore thought he would assist him.

The detective had made up his mind. There was no time to lose; Fogg must be detained at Hong Kong at any price.

"Listen," said Fix sharply; "I am not the agent of the Reform Club as you think."

"Bah!" said Passepartout, looking at him tipsily.

"I am an inspector of police sent out by the authorities from London."

"You are an inspector of police?"

"Yes, I can prove it; here is my authority."

Drawing a paper from his pocket-book, Fix showed his companion his instructions, signed by the Commissioners. Passepartout was dumbfounded.

"This bet of Mr. Fogg's," continued Fix, "is merely a pretence to blind you and his friends at the club, so as to secure your innocent connivance."

"But why?" said Passepartout.

"Listen to me. On the 28th of September last fifty-five thousand pounds was stolen from the Bank of England by a person whose description exactly agrees with Mr. Fogg's appearance."

"Nonsense!" exclaimed Passepartout, striking the table with his clenched fist; "my master is the most honest man in the world."

"What do you know of him?" replied Fix. "You only entered his service on the day he left on this absurd pretext, without luggage, and carrying an immense sum in bank-notes, and yet you dare to maintain that he is an honest man!"

"True, true," replied the lad mechanically.

"Do you want to be arrested as his accomplice?"

Passepartout rested his head between his hands. He was scarcely conscious; he did not dare to look at Fix. Phileas Fogg a robber! that brave, generous man! the rescuer of Aouda a robber! And yet the presumptive evidence against him was strong. Passepartout tried to thrust the suspicion from him; he could not believe his master was guilty.

"Well, what do you want me to do? Speak out!"

"Look here," replied Fix, " I have tracked Fogg so far, but the warrant for his arrest has not yet reached me. You must help me to keep him in Hong Kong."

"I?—but——"

"If so I will share with you the two thousand pounds reward promised by the Bank of England."

"Never!" replied Passepartout as he tried to stand upright, but he fell back quite overcome.

"Mr. Fix," he stammered, "supposing that you have told the truth and that my master is the thief— which I deny—I have been—I am in his service. He has been good and kind to me. I will never betray him for all the gold in the world. I am not that sort of person."

"You refuse?"

"Yes, most decidedly."

"Well, then, let it be as if I had not spoken. Have another glass."

"Yes, all right."

Passepartout felt that he was getting intoxicated, but Fix perceived that he must be separated from his master at any price, to insure success. On the table were some pipes filled with opium. The detective slipped one of these into Passepartout's hand. The lad took it, and after a few puffs fell back completely overcome by the narcotic.

"At last!" said Fix, looking at the senseless figure before him. "Mr. Fogg will not hear of the change of the hour of the steamer's departure, and if he does go he will have to leave this cursed Frenchman behind him."

He then quitted the tavern after paying the score.

CHAPTER XX

Fix encounters Phileas Fogg

While this scene was taking place, and events which gravely compromised Mr. Fogg's future proceedings were passing, that gentleman and Mrs. Aouda were walking through the streets of this English town. She wished to make some purchases for the voyage, and Mr. Fogg overcame all her scruples as to money with his usual generosity.

"It is all in the programme," he replied.

Having made their purchases, they returned to the *table d'hôte* dinner at the hotel. Mrs. Aouda soon afterwards retired, leaving Mr. Fogg to read *The Times* and the *Illustrated London News*.

If Mr. Fogg had been a man to be astonished at anything he would certainly have been astonished at the non-appearance of his servant at bedtime, but thinking that the steamer would not leave Hong Kong before the morning, he did not trouble himself about anything else. But Passepartout did not answer his bell in the morning.

He then learnt that his servant had not come in all night, so Mr. Fogg quietly packed his bag, sent for Mrs. Aouda, and for a palanquin.

It was eight o'clock, and at high-water—namely, at half-past nine—the *Carnatic* was to sail.

Mr. Fogg and Mrs. Aouda got into the palanquin, their baggage came after them, and in half-an-hour they reached the quay, where Mr. Fogg learnt that the *Carnatic* had sailed the night before.

Mr. Fogg, who had counted on finding the steamer and his servant, was obliged to do without either. He showed no disappointment, however, but merely remarked to Mrs. Aouda that it could not be helped.

Just then a person who had been attentively watching him approached. This was Fix, who said:

" Were you not one of the passengers on the *Rangoon*, sir?"

" Yes, sir," replied Mr. Fogg coldly, " but I have not the honour——"

" I beg your pardon, but I expected to find your servant here."

" Do you know where he is, sir?" asked Mrs. Aouda anxiously.

" What!" exclaimed Fix in feigned surprise, " is he not with you?"

" No," she replied; " we have not seen him since yesterday. He may have sailed in the *Carnatic*."

" Without you, madame?" replied the detective. " Excuse me, but you did not intend to leave in that steamer?"

" Yes, sir."

" So did I, madame, and I am greatly disappointed. I understand that the *Carnatic* completed her repairs sooner than was expected, and left Hong Kong twelve hours ago, so we shall have to wait eight days for the next steamer."

Fix was secretly overjoyed as he said these words. In eight days he would receive the warrant of arrest. The chances were now in his favour, but his disgust may be imagined when he heard Phileas Fogg say calmly:

" It appears to me that there are other ships in the

harbour," and offering his arm to Mrs. Aouda, Mr. Fogg walked towards the docks in search of a ship.

Fix followed him as if he were attached to him by a string.

Fortune, however, seemed to have declared against Mr. Fogg. For three hours he searched unsuccessfully for a vessel to take him to Yokohama, but all the ships were either loading or unloading, and could not sail. Fix breathed more freely.

Nevertheless, Mr. Fogg was not disconcerted. He determined to continue his search even if he had to cross to Macao. Just then he was accosted by a sailor.

" Your honour is looking for a boat?" he said, taking off his hat.

" Have you a boat ready to sail?" asked Mr. Fogg.

" Yes, your honour—a pilot-boat, No. 43, the smartest in the fleet."

" She sails fast?"

" About eight or nine knots at least. Would you like to see her?"

" Yes."

" Your honour will be pleased. Do you want her for a trip?"

" No; for a voyage."

" A voyage?"

" I want you to take me to Yokohama if you will."

The sailor folded his arms, and looking at Mr. Fogg, said:

" Your honour is joking."

" No. I have missed the *Carnatic*, and I must be at Yokohama on the 14th to catch the steamer for San Francisco."

" I am very sorry," replied the pilot, " but it can't be done."

" I will give you a hundred pounds a day, and a bonus of two hundred more if you arrive in time."

" Are you serious?" said the pilot.

" Perfectly serious," replied Mr. Fogg.

The pilot walked away a little. He looked earnestly at the sea, evidently hesitating between the desire to gain such a large sum of money and the fear of venturing so far.

Fix was on tenter-hooks all the time.

Meanwhile Mr. Fogg, turning to Aouda, said:

" You are not afraid, I trust?"

" Not with you, Mr. Fogg," she replied.

The pilot then approached, twirling his hat in his hand.

" Well, pilot?" said Mr. Fogg.

" Well, your honour," replied the pilot, " I cannot risk life at this time of year in such a voyage in so small a craft. Besides, we should not reach Yokohama in time. It is one thousand six hundred and fifty miles from Hong Kong to Yokohama."

" Only one thousand six hundred?" said Mr. Fogg.

" Oh, it is all the same."

Fix breathed again.

" However," continued the pilot, " we might arrange it in another way."

Fix scarcely dared to breathe.

" How?" asked Fogg.

" By going to Nagasaki, at the south of Japan, one thousand one hundred miles away, or only to Shanghai, eight hundred miles. In the latter case we can keep close alongshore, and have the advantage of the current northwards."

" It is to Yokohama I want to go," replied Fogg, " to catch the steamer for America, and not to Shanghai or Nagasaki."

" Why not?" replied the pilot. " The San Francisco steamer does not start from Yokohama, but from Shanghai. It only calls at Yokohama and Nagasaki."

" You are sure?"

" Quite sure."

" And when does it leave Shanghai?"

" On the 11th at seven p.m., so we have four days before us. Four days are ninety-six hours, and at eight miles an hour we can reach Shanghai in time if the wind does not drop."

" When can you start?"

" In an hour. I just want to buy some provisions and make ready."

" Well, that's settled. Are you the owner of the boat?"

" Yes, John Bunsby, owner of the *Tankadère*."

" Would you like some money on account?"

" If you have no objection, sir."

" Here are two hundred pounds." Then, turning to Fix, Mr. Fogg said, " If you like to take advantage of this opportunity you can."

" I was about to beg that favour of you," replied Fix.

" Very well; we shall be on board in half-an-hour."

" But about that poor lad?" said Mrs. Aouda, who was anxious about Passepartout.

" I will do all I can," replied Phileas Fogg. And then while the enraged Fix went on board the boat, the other two went to the police-office, where Phileas Fogg gave Passepartout's description, and left a sum of money to pay for a search for him. The same formality was gone through at the French Consulate, and then, having procured their baggage, they proceeded with it on board the ship.

It was three o'clock, and the pilot-boat No. 43 was ready to start. She was a pretty-looking schooner of about twenty tons, built like a racing yacht. All the metal-work was highly polished, and showed that the owner kept her clean and tidy. Her masts raked a little; she carried the usual sails. It was pretty evident she could sail quickly, for she had already gained several prizes in sailing matches.

The owner and four men composed the crew; they were all hardy adventurers, men knowing their business thoroughly. John Bunsby was a man of about five-and-forty, vigorous and energetic, and one capable of inspiring the most timid passengers with confidence.

Phileas Fogg and Mrs. Aouda went on board, where they found Fix; they all went downstairs to the cabin, which was not large, but very neat and comfortable, and lighted by a swinging lamp.

" I regret having nothing better to offer you," said Mr. Fogg to Fix, who bowed without speaking, for he felt rather ashamed of himself.

" Well," he thought, " if he be a thief, he is, at any rate, very polite."

At ten minutes past three the sails were hoisted, the English flag was run up, and Mr. Fogg and Aouda took a last look at the quays in the hope of seeing Passepartout, but they were disappointed.

Fix was rather afraid that the unfortunate lad whom he had treated so badly might appear at the last moment, and that an explanation would ensue which would not redound to the credit of the detective. But the Frenchman did not come, and no doubt he was still under the influence of the narcotic.

So John Bunsby stood out to sea, and the *Tankadère*, with a favourable wind, bounded over the waves.

CHAPTER XXI

In which the owner of the " Tankadère " nearly loses two hundred pounds

This voyage of eight hundred miles was rather a rash undertaking at that time of year in a boat of twenty tons' burden. The China Sea is exposed to high winds, generally about the equinox, and it was then the beginning of November.

It of course would have been greatly to the pilot's advantage to have gone to Yokohama as he was paid by the day, but that would have been too imprudent. It was bad enough to go to Shanghai under the circumstances, but John Bunsby had every confidence in his vessel, and perhaps he was right.

The *Tankadère* proceeded under a press of sail, and behaved admirably.

"There is no necessity for me to urge you to press on," said Fogg to Bunsby when they had got outside.

"Your honour may depend on me," replied the sailor. "We are carrying all the sail we can."

"Well, that's your business; but recollect I trust you thoroughly."

Phileas Fogg, with his legs slightly apart, stood as steadily as a sailor as he gazed over the foaming waves. The young lady was seated aft, and felt somewhat nervous as she contemplated the darkening ocean. Above her head the sails swelled out like great wings, and the schooner made rapid progress.

Night fell, the moon was in her first quarter, and would soon set; heavy clouds were already rising in the east.

The pilot hoisted his lights—a very necessary precaution in those seas, where collisions were frequent—and at the speed she was now going a collision would shatter the schooner to pieces.

Fix kept himself aloof forward, knowing that Fogg was not much of a talker. Besides, he did not wish to enter into conversation with him under the circumstances. He thought of his future movements, as it now appeared certain that Fogg would not stop at Yokohama, but would immediately proceed to San Francisco. His plan appeared to be very simple.

Instead of embarking in England like a common robber, Fogg had made a tour three parts round the globe so as to reach the American continent in safety and enjoy his gains, having thrown the police off the scent. But what could Fix do in America? Was he to abandon the man? No, a hundred times no; he would not lose sight of him till he had obtained a warrant of extradition. This was his duty, and he would do no less. It was fortunate that Passepartout was not now with his master, for after Fix's confidence it was important that the servant should not see Mr. Fogg again.

Phileas Fogg was himself thinking about his servant, and it did not appear to him improbable that the lad had gone on board the *Carnatic* at the last moment. This was Mrs. Aouda's opinion, and the lady much regretted the honest servant's absence. So, after all, they might find Passepartout at Yokohama, and if he had come by the *Carnatic* they could easily ascertain it.

About ten o'clock the wind freshened. Perhaps it would have been prudent to have taken in a reef; but the pilot, after a careful scrutiny of the heavens, let the sails draw. The *Tankadère* carried her canvas very well, but preparations were made to reduce the sail if necessary.

At midnight the passengers retired. The owners and the crew remained on deck all night.

Next morning at sunrise the schooner had made a hundred miles; they were going about eight or nine knots an hour, and at that pace they had every chance of succeeding in their enterprise.

All that day they ran within easy distance of the coast. The wind blew off shore, so the sea was less rough—a very fortunate circumstance as the vessel was of such small tonnage.

About midday the breeze went round to the

south-east, and fell a little. The pilot set his topsails, but took them in again in a couple of hours, for the wind increased.

Mr. Fogg and Mrs. Aouda were spared the horrors of sea-sickness, and ate with appetite. They invited Fix to join them in their repast, and he was obliged to accept but very unwillingly. He felt very uncomfortable to be obliged to travel and eat at the expense of a man he was tracking, but he was obliged to eat, and he did.

However, after dinner he took Mr. Fogg aside, and said, " Sir "—this term Sir stuck in his throat, and he was obliged to control the impulse to collar him— " Sir, it was very kind of you to offer me a passage, but although my means will not allow me to spend money as you do, still I shall be happy to pay my share."

" Don't mention it, sir," replied Mr. Fogg.

" But if I insist?"

" No, sir," replied Fogg in a tone which admitted of no argument. " This is all included in my expenses."

Fix bowed; he felt stifled and went forward, where he sat down and did not speak a word all day.

Meantime they made good way. Bunsby was sanguine, and assured Mr. Fogg they would reach Shanghai in time, to which Mr. Fogg replied that he counted on it. The crew all worked hard, urged by the hope of reward. Not a sheet required bracing, every sail was properly trimmed, and the man at the helm did not permit a single unnecessary lurch. The schooner could not have been sailed better in a match of the Royal Yacht Club Regatta.

In the evening the pilot announced that they had run two hundred and twenty miles from Hong Kong, and Mr. Fogg expected that they would reach Yokohama in good time; if so, the check he had met with would not affect the success of his expedition.

In the early morning the *Tankadère* entered the Strait of Fo-Kien, which separates the island of Formosa from the Chinese shore. The sea was very rough here in consequence of the currents. The schooner rolled very much, and it was difficult for the passengers to keep their feet.

At daybreak the wind freshened still more, and there was every appearance of a storm. The mercury rose and fell capriciously. A long swell came up from the south-east. The sunset the night before had betokened tempest.

The pilot looked anxiously at the sky for some time, and then said to Mr. Fogg:

" May I tell your honour what I think?"

" Tell me everything," replied Mr. Fogg.

" Well, then, we are going to have a storm."

" From what quarter?"

" From the south. Look! a typhoon is approaching."

" If it comes from the south all the better for us," said Mr. Fogg; " it will help us."

" If you take it in that way," replied Bunsby, " I have nothing more to say."

John Bunsby was right. Earlier in the year the typhoon would probably have been dissipated in the form of lightning, but in the winter it would take its own course.

The pilot made all taut. He took in everything but the storm-jib, and waited the result. He begged the passengers to go below, but they objected to the confinement of the cabin and stayed on deck. About eight o'clock the tempest burst with torrents of rain. With only the small sail the *Tankadère* was nearly lifted out of the water, and then she darted onwards like a locomotive at full speed.

All that day the vessel ran before the wind and sea at a tremendous pace. Time after time she nearly broached to, but the steady steering saved her. The passengers were wet to the skin, but took it philosophically. Fix grumbled considerably, however; but the brave Aouda, fixing her eyes on Mr. Fogg, whose coolness she greatly admired, showed herself worthy of him, and braved the tempest at his side. As for Fogg, he accepted the storm as part of his programme.

So far the *Tankadère* was running in a northerly direction, but towards evening the wind veered to the north-west; the vessel, now beam on to the sea, rolled terrifically; it was fortunate she was so solidly built, or she must have succumbed.

As night came on the tempest increased more and more. John Bunsby became anxious, and consulted his crew as to their future proceedings. He then came to Mr. Fogg, and said:

" I think we should run for some port about here."

" So do I," replied Mr. Fogg.

" Ah!" said the pilot, " but which?"

" I only know one," replied Fogg calmly.

" That is——"

" Shanghai."

This answer took the pilot aback, but at last he said :

" Yes, your honour is right: Shanghai it shall be."

So the *Tankadère's* course was not altered.

The night was awful. It was a miracle that the vessel did not founder. On two occasions she was caught in the trough of the sea, but everything was let go, and she righted. Mrs. Aouda was much bruised, but made no complaint. More than once Fogg rushed to her assistance.

At daybreak the storm was still violent, when suddenly the wind backed to the south-east. This was so far favourable that the *Tankadère* rushed over the cross sea which dealt her some fearful blows, which might have crushed a vessel less solidly built.

Occasionally they caught a glimpse of the coast through the mist, but not a sail was visible. The *Tankadère* was alone on the ocean.

At noon the weather showed symptoms of clearing, and improved considerably at sunset; the storm was over, and the passengers could take some rest.

The night was comparatively quiet, more sail was set, and next morning, the 11th, John Bunsby, after an inspection of the coast, declared that they were within a hundred miles of Shanghai.

One hundred miles and only one day left! Mr. Fogg was due at Shanghai that evening, if he would catch the steamer. But for the storm, by which they had lost several hours, they would at that moment be within thirty miles of the port.

The wind dropped, but fortunately the sea went down also. Every stitch of canvas was spread, and at midday the *Tankadère* was only forty-five miles from Shanghai. They had still six hours left.

Everybody on board (except Phileas Fogg) betrayed the greatest anxiety.

To succeed it was necessary to maintain a speed of nine knots an hour, and the wind was now dropping or coming merely in puffs.

However, the vessel was so light and spread so much canvas, and aided as she was by the current, that John Bunsby reckoned at six o'clock that they had only ten more miles to the Shanghai river, for the town itself is situated twelve miles from the mouth.

At seven o'clock they had still three miles to go. A formidable oath escaped the pilot; the bonus of two hundred pounds was slipping from him. He looked at Mr. Fogg. Mr. Fogg was impassible, and yet his whole fortune was staked on the issue. At that moment, too, a high black funnel, crowned with a wreath of black smoke, appeared over the sea. This was the American steamer leaving Shanghai at its correct time.

"Confound it!" cried Bunsby, as he kept the schooner away a bit.

"Make a signal," said Fogg simply.

A small brass cannon was on the forecastle. This little gun was used during fogs.

The piece was charged, but just as the pilot was going to fire it Mr. Fogg told him to hoist the flag.

The ensign was run half-mast high. This was a signal of distress, and they hoped that if those on board the American vessel perceived it they would heave to.

"Fire!" cried Mr. Fogg.

As he spoke the report of the little cannon boomed in the air.

CHAPTER XXII

Passepartout finds out that even at the Antipodes it is useful to have money in his pocket

The *Carnatic* left Hong Kong at half-past six on the evening of the 7th of November, and proceeded for Japan. She carried a full cargo and a large complement of passengers. Two cabins remained unoccupied. They were those retained for Mr. Fogg.

Next morning the crew were surprised to see a dishevelled, half-stupid individual come on deck forward and sit down.

This was Passepartout. And this is how he arrived. After Fix had left the smoking-house Passepartout had remained for three hours insensible upon the couch. He then woke up, and, haunted by the one idea of the steamer, he struggled to rouse himself. The thought of his duty unfulfilled assisted him to throw off his stupor. He left the drunkards' bed, and, guiding his tottering footsteps by the walls, he stumbled on, crying out as in a dream—" The *Carnatic*! the *Carnatic*!"

The steamer was alongside and not far off, quite ready to start. Passepartout staggered across the gangway and fell senseless upon the fore-deck just as the paddles began to revolve.

Some sailors who were accustomed to these scenes carried him downstairs, and Passepartout did not recover until he was one hundred and fifty miles from the Chinese coast.

That is how he got on board the *Carnatic* and why he was now inhaling the sea breezes, which were rapidly sobering him. He tried to collect his thoughts, and at last he remembered the incidents of the previous day.

" It is very evident that I was extremely drunk," he said to himself. " What will Mr. Fogg think? However, I have not missed the ship, and that is a great point."

Then he thought of Fix, and muttered:

" I hope he has not dared to follow us on board, as he said he would. A detective on my master's track, and accused of robbing the Bank of England! Nonsense! Mr. Fogg is no more a robber than I am a murderer."

Passepartout did not know whether he should tell his master what Fix had said. " Would it not rather be better to wait till they got to London, and then have a good laugh at the detective for following them round the world?" At any rate, he would think about it. The first thing was to ask Mr. Fogg's pardon for his unruly conduct.

It was not without difficulty that Passepartout managed to reach the quarter-deck, but there he could not see anyone resembling his master or Mrs. Aouda.

" Oh," he thought, " she is probably not up yet, and Mr. Fogg is no doubt playing whist as usual."

So Passepartout went down to the saloon. Mr. Fogg was not there. There was nothing now for him to do but to inquire for Mr. Fogg's cabin. The steward replied that he did not know the name.

"Excuse me," insisted Passepartout. "The gentleman I mean is tall, very cool and quiet-looking. He is accompanied by a young lady."

"We have no young lady on board," replied the steward. "However, here is the list of passengers. You can look for yourself."

Passepartout read the list. His master's name did not appear in it. He was greatly astonished. At last an idea struck him.

"Is this the *Carnatic*?"

"Yes," replied the steward.

"Bound to Yokohama?"

"Quite so."

Passepartout for an instant had feared that he had gone on board the wrong vessel, but, as he was on board the *Carnatic*, it was evident his master was not.

He fell back into a chair as if he had been shot. He suddenly remembered that the hour of the ship's sailing had been altered, and that he had not informed his master, so he and Mrs. Aouda had missed the ship.

His fault, no doubt, but still more the fault of that rascal who, to separate him from his master and to detain Mr. Fogg at Hong Kong, had made him (Passepartout) tipsy. The detective's object was now evident. Mr. Fogg was no doubt arrested, imprisoned, and ruined. Passepartout tore his hair, and if Fix ever came across him again he promised himself a settlement of accounts.

But he recovered himself and began to look things in the face. They did not look pleasant. He was *en route* to Japan, no doubt, but he had no money, not a penny. Certainly his passage and board had been paid in advance, so he had five or six days to decide what course he should take. Meantime he ate and drank for Mrs. Aouda, his master, and himself, and as if Japan, whither he was bound, was a desert country where nothing could be procured.

On the 13th the *Carnatic* entered the port of Yokohama on the morning's flood tide.

Yokohama is a very important station, where all steamers between America, China, and the islands call in. The town is situated in the same bay as Yeddo, not very far from that large city, the second capital of the Japanese empire, the former residence of the Tycoon.

The *Carnatic* came alongside the quay amidst a crowd of vessels of all nations.

Passepartout went ashore without any curiosity to see this land of the sons of the sun. He had only chance to guide him, and he wandered at random through the streets. He first reached what appeared to be quite a European part of the town, which included all the streets, squares, docks, and warehouses between the promontory of the Treaty and the River. Here, as at Hong Kong and Calcutta were merchants of all nations ready to buy or sell anything amongst whom the Frenchman felt like a Hottentot.

He had, however, one resource: he could apply to the French or English consular agents, but he did not like to tell his adventures, which were so intimately connected with his master, so he thought he would wait to see what turned up. So, having traversed the European quarter without any result, he entered the Japanese district, determined to push on to Yeddo if necessary.

The native quarter of Yokohama is called Benten, after the sea goddess who is worshipped on the neighbouring islands. There are beautiful groves of firs and cedars, sacred gates of strange construction, bridges and temples surrounded by bamboos and melancholy-looking cedars, in the midst of which Buddhist priests and votaries of Confucius live. The interminable streets are crowded with children, apparently cut from Japanese screens, who were playing with short-legged poodles and yellow tailless cats, very lazy and very affectionate.

The streets were filled with people, priests, Custom House officers, bonzes striking their monotonous tambourines, soldiers clothed in blue striped cotton dresses, armed with rifles, the bodyguard of the Mikado, in silk doublets and coats of mail, with numerous other soldiers, for in Japan the soldier is as highly esteemed as he is despised in China. There were friars, pilgrims in long robes, civilians with long hair, large heads, long bodies and thin legs, with pale or copper-coloured complexions, not yellow, like the Chinese, from whom the Japanese differ considerably. Moving about amongst the carriages, palanquins, horses, porters, bamboo litters, Passepartout noticed many good-looking women trotting about with pretty little steps on tiny feet, clad with silken slippers, straw sandals, and wooden clogs. Their eyes were small, they were very flat-chested, their teeth were black, which was fashionable, but they wore the national kirimon, a sort of dressing-gown tied behind with a silk scarf very gracefully, a style of dress which Parisians have borrowed from the Japanese.

Passepartout walked about in the crowd for hours, looking at the glittering shops and bazaars, the restaurants and tea-houses, where they drank saki, a liquor fermented from rice, and the comfortable tobacco-shops, where real tobacco and not opium is smoked, for that drug is almost unknown in Japan. He then passed on amongst the rice plantations, where were flowers of various kinds, beautiful camelias growing on trees, inclosures of bamboo, with cherry, plum, and apple trees, which are cultivated rather for their flower than fruit, and where numbers of birds, eagles and herons, crows, ducks, hawks, and geese were to be seen, and a quantity of cranes, which are held sacred by the Japanese, who think they symbolize long life and happiness.

As he was wandering about Passepartout noticed some violets.

" Ah!" he thought, " here is my supper," but he found they were scentless.

" No chance for me here," he thought.

It was fortunate he had a good meal before he left the *Carnatic*, but now, after wandering about the whole day, he felt very hungry. He had particularly remarked that there was no mutton, nor a kid, nor pork in the shops of the native butchers. He knew it was sacrilege to kill oxen, which are kept for farming purposes, and he therefore concluded that meat was rare in Japan. He was right, but at that time he would not have objected to wild boar, or partridges, quails, chicken, or fish, which the Japanese eat almost exclusively with rice. However, he kept a good heart and looked forward to a meal on the morrow.

Night came on, and Passepartout returned to the native quarter, where he wandered about in the light of coloured lanterns looking at the conjurers and at the astrologers, who had crowds of admirers. Then he wandered on to the harbour, which was lighted up by the torches of the fishermen, who hoped to attract fish to their nets by the light.

At length the streets became deserted. The patrols succeeded the crowd. These officers in their gorgeous uniforms, followed by their suits, resembled ambassadors, and Passepartout, every time he met one of them, said to himself:

"Good; another Japanese embassy is going to Europe."

CHAPTER XXIII
Passepartout's nose gets very long indeed

Next morning Passepartout was very tired and very hungry, and began to think that the sooner he got something to eat the better. He still retained his watch, which of course he could sell, but he thought he would rather die of hunger than do that. It was, however, a case of now or never, and he must use the strong if not melodious voice which Nature had given him.

He knew several French and English songs, and resolved to try. The Japanese must be fond of music since they are always beating tomtoms, cymbals, or drums, and would, no doubt, appreciate European talent.

But perhaps it was rather early to begin singing, and amateurs inopportunely roused might bestow on him more kicks than halfpence, so he decided to wait a few hours, and meantime he thought he would clothe himself in a manner more befitting a wandering minstrel in his position. The exchange also would give him a balance of money wherewith to satisfy his appetite.

Having made up his mind to this project, he immediately put it in execution. After some time he discovered a dealer in old clothes, and soon afterwards Passepartout left the shop attired in a Japanese robe and an old weather-beaten turban; but, on the other hand, he had some money in his pocket.

"I must only imagine myself in fancy dress," he thought.

Passepartout's first act, now that he was a Japanese,

was to enter a tea-house of modest appearance, where, on some fowl and rice, he breakfasted like a man who did not know where his dinner was to come from.

"Now," he thought, when he had eaten fully, "I must make up my mind what I shall do. My only resource is to sell this dress for another of still more Japanese cut. I must leave this Country of the Sun as fast as I can, and I shall not be very sorry to do so."

Passepartout thought that he would go and see what vessels were likely to start to America, for he proposed to work his passage as cook or steward. Once at San Francisco he would be all right. The difficulty was to get across the four thousand seven hundred miles of ocean between Japan and America.

He was not a man to let an idea drop, so he at once went to the docks, where he found his project very difficult of execution. What did they want with a cook or steward on board an American steamer, and what confidence could he inspire? Where were his testimonials and references?

As he was thinking about these things his gaze lighted upon an immense placard which a sort of clown was carrying through the street. The notice was presumably in English, and was as follows:

THE HONOURABLE WILLIAM BATULCAR'S TROUPE OF
JAPANESE ACROBATS
Positively the Last Representation prior to their
Departure for the United States of America of the
LONG NOSES
Under the Special Patronage of the God Tingou
Great Attraction

"The United States of America!" exclaimed Passepartout; "that will suit me very well."

He followed the bearer of the placard into the Japanese quarter of the town, where they soon stopped before a large booth adorned with flags, on the exterior of which were depicted many drawings of acrobats.

This was the Honourable Mr. Batulcar's establishment. This gentleman—a sort of Barnum—was the manager of a troupe of acrobats, clowns, and gymnasts who were giving the last of a series of performances prior to their departure, as the bills set forth.

Passepartout entered and asked for Mr. Batulcar. That gentleman appeared in person.

"What do you want?" he said to Passepartout, whom he took for a native.

"Do you want a servant?" asked the latter.

"A servant!" exclaimed the Barnum, stroking his grey beard. "I have a pair of obedient and faithful servants, who have never left me, and serve me for nothing but their keep, and here they are," he added, indicating his brawny arms, on which the veins stood out like the strings of a double-bass.

"So I can be of no use?"

"Not in the least."

"The devil! It would have suited me very well to have gone to America with you."

"Look here," said Mr. Batulcar, "I expect you are about as much a Japanese as I am an ape. Why have you got yourself up in that style?"

"One must dress as one can."

"That's so. You are a Frenchman, I guess?"

"Yes, a Parisian."

"Well, I suppose you know how to make faces?"

Passepartout was somewhat vexed that his nationality should have provoked such a remark, but he replied, "It is true we can make faces, but no more than Americans do."

"That's a fact. Well, if I take you for my servant I guess you will have to come as a clown. This is how

122

it is—in France, you see, they engage foreign clowns; in foreign countries French clowns."

" Ah ! "

" You are pretty strong, I expect ? "

" Yes; particularly after dinner."

" And you can sing ? "

" Yes," replied Passepartout, who had formerly sung in street concerts.

" But can you sing standing on your head with a top spinning on the sole of your left foot and a sword balanced on your right ? "

" I think so," replied Passepartout, as he recalled the exercises of his youth.

" Well, that's all about it," replied the Honourable Mr. Batulcar, and so the engagement was ratified on the spot.

As it happened, Passepartout got employment.

He was to make one of the celebrated Japanese troupe. This was not aristocratic, but in eight days he would be *en route* for San Francisco.

The performance was to commence at three o'clock, and the orchestra soon assembled. Passepartout had no rehearsal, but he was obliged to make one of a human pyramid executed by the Long Noses of the god Tingou. This was the great attraction, and would close the performance.

Before three o'clock the house was filled with Europeans and natives, Chinese, Japanese, men, women, and children. The orchestra performed a noisy overture as an introduction.

The representation was similar to most acrobatic exhibitions; but it must be confessed that the Japanese are the cleverest of the fraternity. One of them with a fan and some pieces of paper did the graceful butterfly trick. Another with a perfumed smoke of his pipe traced rapidly in the air a

123

compliment to the audience; another juggled with lighted candles which he extinguished successively as they passed his mouth, and then relit them without suspending his sleight-of-hand performance for a moment; another produced a series of combinations with spinning-tops, which he compelled to run along pipe-stems, on the edges of swords, on iron wire, and even on hair stretched across the stage. The tops spun round glass goblets, crossed ladders, ran into corners, and produced harmonic effects as they revolved together. These jugglers played with them, threw them about in the air like shuttlecocks, and put them into their pockets, from which they reproduced them still spinning.

It would be useless to detail all the wonderful performances of the troupe, but the principal attraction was the exhibition by the Long Noses, which has never yet been seen in Europe.

The Long Noses were supposed to be under the immediate patronage of the god Tingou. Clothed like the heroes of the Middle Ages, each individual wore a pair of wings, but were particularly observable for their long noses and the use they made of them. These noses were only bamboo about six or eight feet long. Some were straight, some curved, some were ribbed, some had warts. Now on these noses, which were fixed to their face, they performed their exercises. A dozen of the votaries of Tingou lay upon their backs while their comrades, as stiff as lightning-conductors, jumped from one to the other executing the most wonderful somersaults.

The performance was to terminate with the human pyramid wherein fifty of the Long Noses would represent the " Car of Juggernaut." Instead of making the pyramid on their shoulders the *artistes* mounted on each other's noses. One of them who had represented the base of the car had lately left the troupe, and Passe-partout had been appointed to succeed him.

That worthy felt very melancholy when he donned his costume and fixed his wings to his shoulders and his six-foot nose to his face; but at any rate he had to earn his bread, and he made up his mind to the business.

He went on the stage and arranged with his colleagues the base of the Car of Juggernaut. Some lay flat on the ground, their noses perpendicularly in the air, others mounted upon them, and so on a third and fourth layer almost to the roof of the theatre.

The applause was redoubled, the orchestra played loudly, when suddenly the equilibrium of the pyramid was destroyed—one of the noses at the bottom fell out, and the whole monument collapsed like a house of cards.

It was all the fault of Passepartout, who, leaving his post, leaped over the orchestra without any help from his wings, scaled the right-hand gallery, and, falling at the feet of one of the spectators, cried out:

" Oh, my master! my dear master!"

" Is it you?"

" Yes, it is I."

" Well, then, you had better go on board the steamer, my lad."

Mr. Fogg, Mrs. Aouda, and Passepartout hurried out, but at the door they met the Honourable Mr. Batulcar, who in a terrible rage demanded damages for the fall of the pyramid. Phileas Fogg calmed his fury by throwing him a handful of bank-notes, and at half-past six, punctually, the travellers embarked on the American steamer, followed by Passepartout, who still wore his wings and his long nose, which he had not yet taken off.

CHAPTER XXIV

The Pacific Ocean is safely crossed

It is not difficult to guess what had happened at Shanghai. The signals made by the *Tankadère* had been observed by the steamer, and shortly afterwards, Phileas Fogg having paid the passage-money to the pilot and the bonus of two hundred pounds in addition, went on board the mail for Yokohama.

He reached that place on the 14th of November, and there he learnt, greatly to Mrs. Aouda's satisfaction, and perhaps to his own—though he did not say so—that Passepartout had arrived in the *Carnatic* the day before.

Phileas Fogg immediately set out in search of his servant. In vain he made application at the consular offices, and having traversed the streets in fruitless search, he accidentally entered Batulcar's booth. He would not have recognized Passepartout in his novel costume, but the lad had perceived him. Passepartout could not restrain a twitch of the nose, and thus the accident to the troupe.

Mrs. Aouda told Passepartout what had occurred during his absence, and how they had all come from Hong Kong in the *Tankadère*. Passepartout did not betray any emotion at the mention of Fix's name. He thought the time for explanation to his master had not yet arrived. So he only attributed his absence to a taste of opium in the smoking-house at Hong Kong.

Mr. Fogg listened quietly without remark, and then handed his servant money sufficient to procure him a change of costume, and in about an hour he was dressed " like a Christian " once again.

The steamer was called the *General Grant*, and was a large paddle-wheel vessel belonging to the Pacific

Mail Company. The immense beam-engine rose and fell amidships, and appeared high above the deck. She carried a large spread of canvas, and at twelve knots an hour would cross the ocean in twenty-one days, so Phileas Fogg was justified in believing that he would reach San Francisco on the 2nd of December, New York on the 11th, and London on the 20th, and so gain some hours upon the stipulated time.

There were a good many passengers, English and Americans, coolies bound for the States, and officers on leave from India enjoying their trip round the world.

Nothing of any consequence occurred. There was little or no rolling, for the Pacific justified its name. Mr. Fogg was equally calm and as uncommunicative as usual. Mrs. Aouda was becoming more and more attached to this singular man, and by ties stronger than gratitude; but Mr. Fogg made no sign that he was in any way impressed.

Besides, Mrs. Aouda interested herself greatly in Mr. Fogg's plans. She was very uneasy when anything threatened the success of his journey. She would often talk with Passepartout, and he, guessing how the land lay, always praised his master, and reassured Mrs. Aouda respecting their ultimate success, repeating that the most difficult part of the voyage had been accomplished, that they were returning to civilized countries, and that the train from San Francisco to New York, and the steamer from thence to Liverpool, would, no doubt, bring them home in time.

Nine days after leaving Yokohama Phileas Fogg had gone exactly half-way round the world.

In fact, on the 23rd of November the *General Grant* passed the 180th meridian, which is the antipodes of London. Of the eighty days at his disposal, Mr. Fogg had, it is true, expended fifty-two; but it must be remembered that if he had only gone half-way,

127

according to the difference of the meridian, he had really accomplished two-thirds of his journey. He had made long detours, but by following the 50th parallel, which is that of London, the distance would only have been about twelve thousand miles, whereas by the caprices of the means of locomotion he had actually to cover twenty-six thousand, of which he had now accomplished seventeen thousand five hundred. But now the route was direct, and Fix was not there to put obstacles in his way.

On the 23rd of November Passepartout experienced a great pleasure. It may be remembered that he had obstinately kept London time with his famous family watch, looking upon all other timekeepers as impostors, and on that day he found that his watch exactly agreed with the chronometers on board.

Passepartout was triumphant, and wished Fix had been there that he might remind him of the falsehoods he had told about meridians, the sun and moon. " If we listened to such a fellow as he is," thought Passepartout, " we should keep a nice sort of time. I was quite sure that the sun would regulate itself by my watch sooner or later."

But Passepartout was not aware that if his watch-dial had been divided into the four-and-twenty hours, as the Italian clocks are, he would have no cause for congratulation, as in that case the hands would have pointed to nine o'clock in the evening instead of nine in the morning, as they did on the ship's clocks—that is to say, the one-and-twentieth hour after midnight, which is the exact difference between London time and that at the 180th meridian.

But if Fix had been capable of explaining the physical effect, Passepartout, even if he had understood it, would not have confessed it, and it is probable that if the detective had been then on board,

Passepartout would have engaged him on a different subject, and in a very different manner.

Now where was Fix at this moment?

He was on board the *General Grant*.

When Fix reached Yokohama he at once left Mr. Fogg and proceeded to the English consulate; there he actually found the warrant which had come by the *Carnatic*, on board of which steamer they thought he had arrived. The disappointment of the detective can be imagined. The warrant was now useless, as Fogg was no longer on English territory. A writ of extradition would now be necessary to arrest him.

" It can't be helped," thought Fix when his anger had subsided. " The warrant is no use here, but it will be in England. The fellow is evidently returning home, thinking he has thrown the police off the scent, but I will follow him all the way, though goodness knows how much money will be left. He must have spent, in one way or another, about five thousand pounds already, but the Bank can afford it."

So he embarked on the *General Grant*, and saw Mr. Fogg and Mrs. Aouda arrive. To his great surprise he recognized Passepartout in his curious dress, but Fix immediately hid himself in his cabin to avoid a chance meeting, and hoped he would remain unperceived during the voyage. But that very day he came face to face with Passepartout on the fore-deck.

Without any explanation Passepartout caught him by the throat, and, greatly to the delight of certain Americans who bet on the result, he administered a considerable thrashing to the detective, and demonstrated the superiority of the French system of boxing.

When Passepartout had finished this little exercise he felt much refreshed. Fix got up in a very dishevelled condition, and, looking coolly at his adversary, said:

" Have you finished?"

" Yes, for the present."

" Then come and speak to me."

" What——?"

" It is in your master's interest."

Passepartout, overcome by this coolness, followed the detective, who said:

" You have given me a licking. All right, but just now listen to me. Till now I have been Mr. Fogg's enemy; for the future I will assist him."

" Ah, so you believe him honest?" said Passepartout.

" No," replied the detective, " I think he is a thief. Be quiet and listen to me. As long as Mr. Fogg was on English territory I had an interest in endeavouring to detain him till the warrant for his arrest reached me, and did all in my power to stop him. It was I who put the Bombay priests on your track. I drugged you at Hong Kong, separated you from your master, and caused him to lose the steamer to Yokohama."

Passepartout involuntarily clenched his fists as he listened.

" Now," Fix continued, " Mr. Fogg appears desirous of returning to England. Very well, I will follow him. But in future I will do all I can to clear the way for him with as much pleasure as I have hitherto put obstacles in his way. You see I have changed my tactics, for my own interests of course. I may say that your interest is identical with mine, for in England only will you be able to ascertain whether your master is a criminal or an honest man."

Passepartout had listened attentively, and was convinced that Fix spoke in good faith.

" Are we friends?" said Fix.

" Friends? No," replied Passepartout. " Allies, if you please, to a certain extent, for at the least sign of treason I will wring your neck."

" Agreed," said Fix calmly.

Eleven days afterwards—namely, on the 3rd of December—the *General Grant* entered the Golden Gate, and arrived at San Francisco.

Mr. Fogg had neither gained nor lost a day as yet.

CHAPTER XXV

A glimpse of San Francisco—a meeting

It was seven o'clock in the morning when Phileas Fogg, Mrs. Aouda, and Passepartout landed on the American continent, if the floating pier can be so designated. These landing-places, rising and falling with the tide, facilitate the loading and unloading of vessels, which were there in every variety and size, including steam ferry-boats with many decks, which ply on the Sacramento and its tributaries. There were also amassed the products of all nations from Europe to the Pacific, Peru, Chili, and Brazil.

Passepartout was so delighted to land in America that he thought it proper to leap on shore in his best style, but when he alighted on the quay he found it was worm-eaten, and he went through it. Very much discouraged, he cried out for assistance, and frightened all the cormorants and pelicans in the neighbourhood.

As soon as Mr. Fogg landed he proceeded to ascertain when the train started for New York. It was to leave at six o'clock, so the travellers had a whole day before them. Mr. Fogg took a carriage and drove with his companions to the *International Hotel*.

Passepartout sat upon the box, and gazed with curiosity upon this large American town, with its wide streets and lofty houses, its churches built in the Anglo-Saxon Gothic style, its immense docks and warehouses, and innumerable cabs, omnibuses, and tramcars. Americans, Europeans, Chinese, and Indians jostled each other on the pathway, and made up the population to a total of 200,000.

Passepartout was astonished at all he saw. San Francisco was no longer such a town as it was in 1849, a resort of bandits, incendiaries, and assassins, a population who gambled for gold-dust, a knife in one hand and a revolver in another. These good times had passed by, and San Francisco was respectable. The high tower of the city hall overlooked the streets, which crossed each other at right angles, with green squares between, while the Chinese quarter looked like a section of the Celestial Empire imported in a puzzle. Sombreros, red shirts, and Indian plumed headdresses were no longer to be seen; silk hats and black coats were worn by most people, and some of the principal streets—for instance, Montgomery Street, which is the Regent Street of San Francisco—was lined with magnificent shops, offering for sale the products of the world.

When Passepartout had arrived at the *International Hotel* he fancied himself in England, though the ground floor of the hotel was occupied by an immense bar, where there was a free lunch of cold meat, oyster soup, biscuit and cheese, though stimulants had to be paid for. This institution was certainly very American.

The restaurant at the hotel was very comfortable. Mr. Fogg and Mrs. Aouda sat down at a table, where they were served on very small plates by the blackest of negroes.

After breakfast Phileas Fogg, accompanied by Mrs. Aouda, went to the English Consulate to have his passport *viséd*. On the way he met his servant, who asked hi mif he had not better purchase some firearms, for Passepartout had heard of trains being attacked by the Indians. Mr. Fogg thought the precaution needless, but told him he might do as he pleased.

The travellers had not gone far on their way to the Consulate when, "by a most extraordinary coincidence," they met Fix who appeared extremely surprised. Was it really true that he and Mr. Fogg had crossed the Pacific in the same ship and had not met on board? Fix professed himself greatly honoured at meeting this gentleman again, and, as his business called him to Europe again, he would be only too delighted to travel in such company.

Mr. Fogg replied that the honour was on his side, and Fix, who had determined not to lose sight of Mr. Fogg, asked permission to accompany him, and his request was granted.

So the trio walked about, and soon reached Montgomery Street, where there was a tremendous crowd. On the pavement, in the roadway and tramway, notwithstanding the incessant movement of vehicles, people were everywhere walking about, while others at the windows, and even on the roofs of the houses, were shouting and waving great flags and streamers, and all were calling out, "Hurrah for Camerfield!" or "Hurrah for Mandiboy!" It was a meeting, Fix thought, and said to Mr. Fogg that they had better not mingle with the crowd for fear of getting hustled.

Mr. Fogg assented, and said that blows, even inflicted for political reasons, were nevertheless blows.

Fix thought he ought to smile, and accordingly did so, and then, in order to see what was going on, they mounted on the top of some steps. Opposite them was a platform, towards which the crowd was converging.

But what the object of this meeting was Fogg could not determine, and just then the excitement became tremendous; hands were held up in the air; some were clenched, as if ready to fight or to register a vote. The crowd swayed backwards and forwards, the banners were agitated, and almost immediately were torn into shreds. The crowd advanced towards the steps, hats were smashed, and every individual appeared to have grown shorter.

"It is evidently a political question," said Fix. "I should not be surprised if it were about the Alabama business, though that is already settled."

"Perhaps so," replied Mr. Fogg simply.

"However, here are the candidates," continued Fix. "The honourable gentlemen have met."

Mrs. Aouda, clinging to Mr. Fogg's arm, regarded the tumult with astonishment, and Fix was about to ask the reason of it all when the excitement suddenly increased. People became more violent, the shouts and cries redoubled, the poles of the banners were used as weapons, hands and fists seemed ubiquitous, all traffic was stopped, blows were exchanged, boots and shoes were converted into missiles, and the ominous detonation of revolvers was heard.

The crowd was approaching the steps near the travellers. It was evident that one of the parties had been defeated, but no one could tell which.

"I think it would be more prudent to retire," said Fix, who only thought that his prey might escape him. "If any question arise about England, and we are recognized, it might not be so pleasant."

"An Englishman——" said Mr. Fogg.

But he never finished his sentence. Behind them the uproar rose louder than ever; there were shouts for Mandiboy, a party of whose friends had come to the rescue, and were attacking the partisans of Camerfield by a flank movement.

Mr. Fogg and his friends were now between two fires. It was too late to escape. The armed crowd could not be withstood. Mr. Fogg and Fix did all in their power to protect Mrs. Aouda, but they were

tremendously knocked about. Mr. Fogg tried to
practise his boxing, but a tall ruffian with a red beard,
who was apparently the chief of the band, levelled a
blow at Mr. Fogg, and would have severely injured
him had not Fix interposed and received the blow, by
which his hat was completely knocked out of shape.

" You low Yankee!" exclaimed Mr. Fogg with profound contempt.

" You darned Britisher!" replied the other.

" We shall meet again."

" Whenever you like. What's your name?"

" Phileas Fogg. What's yours?"

" Colonel Stamp W. Proctor."

Then the surging crowd passed on, and Fix, who
had been overturned, rose to his feet; his clothes were
much torn, but he was not otherwise injured. Fortunately Mrs. Aouda had escaped as well as Mr. Fogg.

" Thank you," said that gentleman to the detective
when they got clear of the crowd.

" Oh! that's nothing," replied Fix; " come along."

" Where to?"

" To a tailor."

Indeed it was necessary, for the clothes of both men
were as badly torn as if they had been fighting for one
or other of the candidates.

An hour afterwards they were sitting newly clothed
in the *International Hotel*.

There Passepartout appeared armed with half-a-
dozen central fire revolvers. When he saw Fix he was
much annoyed, but when Mrs. Aouda told him what
had happened he felt more amiable. Fix was evidently no longer an enemy, and would keep his word.

After dinner they took a coach and drove to the
railway station with their luggage. As they were
getting into the station Mr. Fogg said to Fix:

" Have you seen that Colonel Proctor again?"

" No," replied Fix.

" I will come back to America for the purpose of finding him out," said Fogg coolly. " No Englishman should submit to be treated as he has treated me."

Fix smiled, but did not answer. He saw, however, that Mr. Fogg was one of those Englishmen who, disapproving of duelling at home, will fight when they are abroad if their honour is in question.

At a quarter to six the travellers reached the railway station and found the train ready to start.

As he got into the carriage Mr. Fogg asked a porter what was the cause of the excitement that day.

" It was a meeting, sir," replied the man.

" I noticed that there was a very great commotion in the town."

" It was only an election meeting," replied the man.

" For a commander-in-chief I suppose!" said Mr. Fogg.

" No, sir, for a justice of the peace!"

When he heard this Mr. Fogg got into the train, which started almost immediately after.

CHAPTER XXVI

The Express train on the Pacific Railway

From ocean to ocean, as the Americans say, and these words appear to be the general denomination of the Grand Trunk Railway across the States, but in reality the line is divided into two distinct portions—the Central Pacific, between San Francisco and Ogden, and the Union Pacific, thence to Omaha. There are five different railways between Omaha and New York.

Thus New York and San Francisco are united by a continuous line not less than three thousand seven hundred and eighty-six miles in length. Between Omaha and the Pacific the railroad crosses a country still inhabited by Indians and wild beasts—a vast extensive territory which the Mormons began to colonize in 1845 after they had been driven from Illinois.

Formerly, under the most favourable circumstances, six months were occupied in crossing the continent. Now it is traversed in seven days.

It was in 1862 that, notwithstanding the opposition of the Southern deputies, who wished the line to run farther south, the railroad was planned between the 41st and 42nd parallels of latitude. President Lincoln himself fixed the termination of the line at Omaha. The work was immediately begun, and continued with American energy, which is neither red-tapish nor bureaucratic. The rapidity of the workmanship did not affect its solidity. In the prairie they laid a mile and a half of line a day. A locomotive running on the track laid the day before carried the rails for the following day, and so on, as soon as they were fixed.

The Pacific Railroad has many branches in Iowa, Kansas, Colorado, and Oregon. When it leaves Omaha the line runs along the left bank of the Platte River to the mouth of the northern branch. Then following the southern stream it crosses Laramine territory and the Wahsatch Mountains to Salt Lake City, the Mormon capital. It then plunges into the valley of Tuilla, along the American desert, by Mount Cedar and Humboldt, the Humboldt River and Sierra Nevada, and then redescends by Sacramento to the Pacific, the gradient all the way never exceeding a hundred and twelve feet to the mile, even over the Rocky Mountains.

This was the long artery upon which Phileas Fogg hoped to reach New York in seven days and catch the Liverpool steamer on the 11th of the month.

The car in which Phileas Fogg was seated was a sort

137

of long omnibus resting on bogie trucks, with four wheels at each end, which permitted them to run over very sharp curves; there were no compartments in this carriage, but the seats were arranged in rows on each side, the passage running between them extended throughout the train and gave access to any other of the carriages; there were drawing-room cars, smoking cars, restaurants, and lavatories; the only thing wanting was the theatre car; no doubt that will be arranged some day. Boys selling books and papers, refreshments and tobacco, were continually passing through the carriages.

The travellers left Oakland at six p.m. It was quite dark and cold; snow-clouds covered the sky. The train only ran at about twenty miles an hour, including stoppages. There was not much conversation in the carriages, and the travellers soon went to sleep. Passepartout was close to Fix, but neither of them spoke as their friendship had decidedly cooled, though, to do Fix justice, it was not so much his fault as that of Passepartout, who would have strangled his former friend at the least suspicion.

Snow began to fall about an hour after they started, but not in sufficient quantity to impede their progress. The country looked as if it were covered with an immense tablecloth, against which the steam of the locomotive appeared grey.

At eight o'clock the steward came in. It was bed-time, and in a few moments the carriage was transformed into a sleeping car; the backs of the seats were pulled out, and berths were quickly improvised. Thus each passenger was provided with a bed, protected from observation by curtains. The sheets were clean, the pillows soft. There was nothing to do but go to bed, and everyone did so while the train rushed on through California.

The ground between San Francisco and Sacramento is not hilly. This portion of the line is called the Central Pacific, and runs in an easterly direction from Sacramento to meet the line from Omaha. From San Francisco to the capital of California the line goes north-east along the American river. The hundred and twenty miles between those cities were accomplished in six hours, but as everybody was asleep when they passed through Sacramento no one saw anything of the city.

From Sacramento the railroad runs through the Sierra Nevada range, and the train passed Cisco at seven o'clock. An hour afterwards the sleeping car was again transformed to its original appearance, and the travellers gazed through the windows at the mountainous country. The railroad followed all the caprices of the Sierra, sometimes suspended over precipices, rounding sharp angles, and dashing through narrow gorges which appear to have no end. The engine, its fire gleaming and vomiting black smoke, the warning bell kept ringing, and the cow-catcher extending in front like a great spur, mingled its whistlings and groanings with the roar of a waterfall, while the smoke twisted round the pine-trees.

There are very few tunnels or bridges, for the railroad runs up the mountain, and does not cut through it.

About nine o'clock the train entered the State of Nevada by the Carson Valley, and stopped twenty minutes at Reno for luncheon.

They quitted it at twelve o'clock, and then, coasting the Humboldt River, they pursued an easterly course and followed the river to the Humboldt Ranges, on the eastern side of the State.

After luncheon Mr. Fogg and his companions took their places in the train, and admired the varied scenery. Sometimes a great troop of buffaloes would appear on the horizon. These droves often prevent the progress of the train, for they frequently cross the tracks thousands deep, and occupy several hours in their passage, so the locomotive is forced to stop and wait till the line is clear.

Indeed, this is just what happened on that occasion. About three o'clock in the afternoon a drove blocked the line. The engine-driver moderated his speed and tried to pass through the mass, but could not succeed.

The passengers could see the buffaloes, as they are improperly termed by the Americans, marching quietly across the line, sometimes bellowing loudly. They were bigger than the European bull; the legs and tail are short, the head and shoulders are covered with a long mane, beneath which a muscular hump rises. It is impossible to stop their migration. When the bisons have made up their minds to go in a certain direction, nothing can turn them from it. They are a torrent which it is impossible to dam.

All the travellers gazed at this novel sight, but the man most interested of all remained calmly in his place. Phileas Fogg waited philosophically till the bisons had passed by. Passepartout was furious at the delay, and wanted to discharge his arsenal of revolvers among them.

" This is a pretty sort of country," he said, " when a train can be stopped by a herd of cows, which do not hurry themselves in the least. I wonder if Mr. Fogg expected *this*. The engine-driver is afraid to run against the animals."

The engine-driver certainly had very prudently not attempted to do so. He might, perhaps, have killed two or three of the buffaloes, but the locomotive would quickly have jumped off the track, and the train would have remained helpless.

140

The only thing to do was to wait patiently, in the hope of making up the time when the buffaloes had gone by. But the long line of bisons took three hours to pass, and the line was not clear before dark. Ere this the head of the column of buffaloes had disappeared below the southern horizon.

It was already eight o'clock when the train cleared the defiles of the Humboldt Range. At half-past nine it entered Utah, the Great Salt Lake region, and the curious Mormon territory.

CHAPTER XXVII

Passepartout goes through a course of Mormon history at the rate of twenty miles an hour

During the night the train ran due south for fifty miles, and then turned north-east towards Salt Lake.

Passepartout, about nine o'clock, went out on the platform to get some fresh air. The weather was cold, the sky was grey, but there was no snow. The misty sun looked like an enormous gold plate, and Passepartout was calculating its worth in English money when he was disturbed by the appearance of a curious-looking person.

He was a man who got into the train at Elko, was tall and dark, and clothed almost entirely in black. His necktie was white, and his gloves were of dogskin. He looked like a minister. He passed from car to car, fastening a small bill on every door. Passepartout learnt from one of these that Elder William Hitch, a Mormon missionary, would improve the occasion in Car 117 at eleven o'clock, and invited anyone who wished to hear about the Latter-Day Saints to attend.

" I'll go," thought Passepartout, whose ideas of Mormonism only extended to polygamy.

The news spread rapidly amongst the passengers,

who numbered one hundred, about thirty of whom attended the lecture. Passepartout sat in the front row, but neither his master nor Fix appeared.

At the advertised time Mr. Hitch rose, and in an irritated manner, as if he had been lately contradicted, exclaimed:

"I tell you that Joe Smith is a martyr, and so is his brother Hiram, and that the persecution of the Government will make a martyr of Brigham Young also. Now who will dare to assert the contrary?"

Nobody did, and the excitement of the missionary contrasted strangely with his naturally calm features. No doubt his anger was attributable to the sense of the indignities to which the Mormons had been exposed by the Government of the United States, which had had a great deal of trouble with these fanatics. But the law had prevailed, and had imprisoned Brigham Young on the charge of rebellion and polygamy. Since that time the disciples of the prophet had redoubled their efforts, and by words, if not by deeds, resisted the acts of Congress. So Elder Hitch was trying to gain converts in the cars.

He began his lecture with the history of Mormonism at the time of the patriarchs. He told his audience how that in Israel a Mormon prophet of the tribe of Joseph published the new religion, and left the annals to his son Morom; how many centuries later a translation of this precious book, written in Egyptian characters, had been made by Joseph Smith, junior, a farmer of Vermont, who revealed himself as a prophet in 1825, and how afterwards an angel had appeared in a luminous forest and given him the Sacred Book.

Some of the audience now began to leave the car, but the lecturer proceeded to relate how Smith, with his relatives and a few disciples, founded the religion of the Latter-Day Saints, which counts its converts not only in America but all over Europe, amongst all sorts and conditions of men. The lecturer told how this colony was established in Ohio, where the temple was built which cost two hundred thousand dollars, and built a town at Kirkland; how Smith became a successful banker, and " received from a simple exhibitor of mummies the papyrus scroll written by Abraham and other celebrated Egyptians."

This narrative became very tiresome, and the audience thinned rapidly, but the lecturer nevertheless continued the history of Joe Smith, his bankruptcy, his tarring and feathering, his reappearance (more honourable than ever) in Missouri at the head of about three thousand disciples; and, finally, his pursuit by the Gentiles to the extreme Far West.

By this time only ten of the audience remained, including Passepartout, who was most attentive, and the lecturer continued showing how Smith reappeared in Illinois, and founded the city of Nauvoo in 1839; how he became Mayor and put up for the presidency of the United States; how he was enticed into an ambuscade and assassinated.

Passepartout was now the only listener, and the elder went on to tell him of the actions of the pious Brigham Young, and wound up by saying that the jealousy of Congress was roused against the Mormons because they were flourishing.

" But shall we yield to force? Never! Driven from Vermont, Illinois, Ohio, Missouri, and Utah, we shall still find an independent territory where we can pitch our tent, and you, my faithful friend," added the elder, " will you not rally to our flag?"

" No," replied Passepartout, as he walked away.

Meantime the train had reached the north-west extremity of Salt Lake. From that point the Dead Sea, as it is sometimes called, into which an American

Jordan flows, was fully visible. It is still of immense size, though its former limits have been somewhat reduced.

The Salt Lake is seventy miles long and thirty-five miles wide, and is three thousand eight hundred feet above the level of the sea. It is very different from Lake Asphaltites, though it contains a large quantity of salt; fish cannot live in it, but it is not true that the water is too dense for men to swim in.

All round the Lake the country is well cultivated, for the Mormons are excellent farmers, and six months later corn and maize and abundance of flowers would have rendered the scene most attractive. When our travellers saw it, however, the ground was powdered with snow.

At two o'clock the train reached Ogden, and as it did not leave again till six, Mr. Fogg and his party had time to visit the City of the Saints, where they passed two hours. It is built with the melancholy sadness of right angles, as Victor Hugo expresses it. In this it resembles all cities in the Union, where everything is supposed to be on the square, though individuals do not rise to that height.

At three o'clock our travellers were in the city, which is built between the bank of the Jordan and the Wahsatch Mountains. They noticed very few churches, but the public buildings included the house of the prophet, the court-house, and the arsenal. There were houses of blue brick, with porches and verandas inclosed in gardens planted with palm-trees and acacias. A wall runs round the city. The market-place and several hotels are in the principal street.

The city did not appear to have many inhabitants. The streets were almost deserted, except near the temple. There were a great number of women, as was to be expected, but all the Mormons are not poly-gamists. They are unfettered on this point, but the women are anxious to be married, as only wives are admitted to the full membership of the Church. The poor women appeared neither happy nor comfortable. The richest of them were well-dressed in European style, but the others were merely clothed *à la Indienne*.

Passepartout was somewhat awestricken with these ladies, but, above all, he pitied the husbands. It appeared to him a terrible thing to have to answer for so many women, and lead them to their Mormon para-dise to meet the glorified Smith, who was, no doubt, an ornament to that place, wherever it is. Passepar-tout evidently thought that Mormonism would not suit him, and he fancied—though he might have been mistaken—that some of the ladies gazed at him in a disquieting manner.

Fortunately his stay in the City of the Saints was short. Just before four the travellers returned to the train. As it began to move a voice was heard crying out: "Stop! stop!"

But the engineer proceeded. The man who cried out was a Mormon. He ran till quite out of breath. Fortunately for him the station had no gates nor barriers. He ran along, and succeeded in reaching the platform of the last carriage, and threw himself panting into a seat.

Passepartout, who had been anxiously watching the pursuit, was more particularly interested when he heard that the man had run away after some domestic dispute.

When the Mormon had recovered his breath, Passe-partout ventured to ask him politely how many wives he had, for he fancied, by the haste he had made, that the man must have had twenty at least.

"Only one, sir," replied the Mormon, raising his

arms to heaven. "One, and she is quite enough, I assure you."

CHAPTER XXVIII

Passepartout cannot make anyone listen to reason

When the train left the Great Salt Lake and Ogden it proceeded northwards to the Weber River, having made nine hundred miles from San Francisco, thence it went eastwards across the Wahsatch Mountains. It is here that the engineers had found the greatest difficulty and the Government subsidy had been raised to forty-eight thousand instead of sixteen thousand dollars a mile, as on the plains, but the engineers had turned all difficulties, and had only cut one tunnel of fourteen thousand feet.

At Salt Lake the train reached its highest point, and then curved towards the valley of Bitter Creek, to remount again to the watershed between the Atlantic and the Pacific. There were numerous creeks in this part of the world. There is Muddy Creek, Green Creek, and others were passed on culverts. Passepartout had become more impatient as they approached the end of the journey, and Fix would also have been glad to have got out of this difficult country, for he feared delays and accidents, and was more anxious to reach England than Fogg himself.

At ten o'clock p.m. the train stopped at Fort Bridger, and twenty miles further on it entered the State of Wyoming or Dakota. The next day, the 7th of December, they stopped for a quarter of an hour at Green River. Sleet had fallen during the night, and this weather annoyed Passepartout very much, as a fall of snow would prevent them continuing their journey.

"How absurd it is," he thought, "for my master to
146

have come on such an expedition in winter! If he had waited till the summer he would have had a much better chance."

But while the honest fellow was pre-occupied about the weather Mrs. Aouda was alarmed for an entirely different reason.

The fact was, she had recognized among the passengers Colonel Stamp Proctor, who had so insulted Phileas Fogg at San Francisco.

This circumstance impressed her deeply. She had become attached to the man who, notwithstanding his cold exterior, showed her so much attention. She herself probably did not understand the depth of feeling with which he inspired her, and which she believed to be gratitude, but it was something more than that. When she recognized Mr. Fogg's enemy, her heart almost ceased to beat. No doubt it was by mere accident that they were travelling by the same train, but in any case they must be kept apart.

She took an opportunity, when Mr. Fogg was asleep, to tell Fix and Passepartout how matters stood.

" So Proctor is here, is he?" said Fix. " Well, then, madame, you may be quite easy. He will have to settle with me before he settles with Mr. Fogg, for I received the deepest insults."

" And I shall have something to say to him also," said Passepartout, " colonel though he be."

" Mr. Fix," replied Mrs. Aouda, " Mr. Fogg is not the man to let anybody fight his battle. He has said that he will return to America to meet this man. If he sees him now, we cannot prevent an encounter which may have the most deplorable results. They must be kept apart."

" You are right, madame," replied Fix. " A meeting would spoil everything. Mr. Fogg would be delayed, and——"

" And," added Passepartout, " that would play into the hands of the gentlemen of the Reform Club. Well, in four days we shall be in New York, and if my master does not leave the car in the meantime, he is not likely to meet that confounded American. At any rate, we will do our best to prevent it."

The conversation ceased, for Mr. Fogg awoke. A little later Passepartout whispered to the detective:

" Would you really fight for him?"

" I would do anything to get him back to Europe alive," replied Fix in a determined tone.

Passepartout shuddered, but his faith was firm in his master's rectitude.

Now the question was, how to keep Mr. Fogg in the carriage. It did not appear to be very difficult, for Mr. Fogg was naturally of a sedentary habit, and by no means of an inquisitive turn of mind. But the detective found a way, and accordingly said to Mr. Fogg:

" Time passes very slowly, sir."

" Yes," he replied, " but it passes somehow."

" On board the steamer," continued Fix, " you used to like a rubber of whist."

" Yes," replied Fogg; " but here it would be difficult: there are no cards nor partners."

" Oh, we can easily buy cards, and if madame can take a hand——"

" Certainly, sir," replied the young lady quickly. " I know whist; it is part of an English education."

" I do not know much about it myself," said Fix, " but still we can play ' dummy.' "

" By all means," replied Phileas Fogg, who was delighted at the prospect of a game, even in a railway carriage.

Passepartout was sent for some cards, and soon returned with two packs and markers, and a board covered with cloth. The play began. Mrs. Aouda was a very fair player, and was frequently complimented by Phileas Fogg. Fix was evidently a first-rate hand, and a worthy opponent of that gentleman.

"Ah!" thought Passepartout, "now we have got him down he is not likely to move."

At eleven o'clock in the morning the train reached Bridge Pass, and after traversing another two hundred miles they entered upon one of those vast plains which made the laying of the railway a comparatively easy task.

At half-past twelve the train passed Fort Halleck, which overlooks the district, and shortly afterwards the Rocky Mountains were crossed. Everyone began now to hope that the journey would be accomplished without accident; the snow had ceased, the weather was dry and cold. Some large birds, alarmed by the passing of the train, flew rapidly away, but there was no sign of any other living creature in all the extent of the plain.

After a comfortable breakfast in the train, Mr. Fogg and his partners were about to resume their whist, when the engine-driver whistled loudly and the train stopped.

Passepartout put his head out, but there was no station in sight. Mrs. Aouda and Fix were afraid that Mr. Fogg would leave the train, but he contented himself by telling his servant to see what was the matter.

Passepartout jumped out, and amongst the passengers who had already alighted he found Colonel Stamp Proctor.

The train had been stopped by signal, the engine-driver and guard had got down and were talking to the signalman, who had been sent from Medicine-Bow, the next station. The passengers came up to listen, and Passepartout joined them.

149

As he approached he heard the signalman say: " It is impossible to go. The bridge at Medicine-Bow is out of repair and will not bear the weight of the train."

This viaduct was a suspension bridge carried over a cañon about a mile ahead of the train. As the signal-man said, some of the supports were broken, and it was impossible to cross. He had not exaggerated the danger; and, as a rule, when an American is prudent, it may be taken for granted that rashness will not pay.

Passepartout was afraid to tell his master, and remained listening to the conversation.

" This is all very well," said Colonel Proctor, " but we are not going to stop here to take root in the snow."

" We have telegraphed to Omaha for a train," replied the guard, " but it is not likely it will reach Medicine-Bow for six hours."

" Six hours!" exclaimed Passepartout.

" Yes, sir," replied the conductor; " but we shall want all that time to walk to the station."

" To walk!" cried all the passengers.

" How far is it to the station?"

" About twelve miles from the other side of the river."

" Twelve miles in the snow!" roared Colonel Proctor.

Here the colonel broke into a volley of oaths, which included the company and the conductor, and Passepartout was very nearly agreeing with him. All his master's money could not remove this obstacle.

The disappointment was general, for the passengers would have to walk fifteen miles in the snow. The disturbance would have attracted Phileas Fogg's attention if he had not been so absorbed in his whist.

However, Passepartout would have been obliged to tell him, if the engine-driver, a true Yankee, named Foster, had not made a suggestion.

" Gentlemen," he said, " I think there is a way over."

" Over the bridge?" asked a passenger.

" Yes, sir."

" With the train?" said the colonel.

" Yes."

Passepartout listened intently.

" But the bridge is almost broken down," said the guard.

" No matter," replied Foster. " I think if we put on the full pressure we might rush across."

" The devil!" said Passepartout.

But the suggestion recommended itself to a number of the passengers. Colonel Proctor was particularly pleased, and thought the thing quite easy. He even went so far as to relate certain experiences of his own in which engineers, he said, had crossed rivers, when there were no bridges at all, by merely putting on full steam. The result was that many passengers agreed with the engine-driver.

" The chances are fifty to one," said one.

" Sixty," said another.

" Eighty, ninety to a hundred."

Passepartout was struck dumb, and although he was quite ready to cross the creek, he thought the plan suggested a trifle too American.

" Besides," he thought, " there is an easier way, and nobody seems to have thought about it," so he said to one of the passengers: " Sir, I think the plan proposed is a very rash one, but——"

" Eighty to one," replied the traveller, turning his back upon him.

" I quite understand that," replied Passepartout, " but an idea——"

" Ideas are no good," replied the American, shrugging his shoulders. " The engineer says we can cross."

"No doubt," replied Passepartout, "but it would be more prudent——"

"Who is talking of prudence?" exclaimed Proctor, who was ready to quarrel with anybody for this suggestion. "We are going at full speed—do you understand, at full speed?"

"I understand," said Passepartout, who found it impossible to finish his sentence, "but it would be, if not prudent, as you object to the word, at least more natural——"

"What! what! what! who is talking about being natural?" exclaimed the passengers.

Poor Passepartout could not obtain a hearing.

"Are you afraid?" asked Colonel Proctor.

"Afraid! I?" exclaimed Passepartout. "Ah! I will show you that a Frenchman can be as good as an American any day."

"All aboard?" cried the guard.

"Yes, all aboard," muttered Passepartout, "and what then? But you won't prevent my thinking that it would be more natural for us to cross the bridge, and let the train come after."

But no one heard this sensible remark, and if it had been heard its justice would not have been acknowledged.

The travellers, including Passepartout, re-entered the train without saying what had happened. The whist-players were still deeply engaged.

Then the engine-driver whistled and backed the train for nearly a mile; then, whistling again, he started forwards. The pace became fearful. Nothing was heard but the beatings of the pistons, and the wheels flew round at the speed of nearly one hundred miles an hour. The train scarcely seemed to touch the rails.

The bridge was passed like a flash of lightning.

Nobody saw anything of it. The train leaped, so to speak, from one bank to the other, and could not be pulled up till it had run about five miles beyond the station.

But scarcely had the train passed over the bridge when the structure fell with a tremendous crash into the rapids of Medicine-Bow.

CHAPTER XXIX

Which relates certain incidents which are never met with except on American railroads

The same evening the train proceeded, and passing Fort Saunders and the Cheyenne Pass, reached Evans's Pass. At this point the railroad reached its greatest elevation, which is eight thousand and ninety feet above the sea. The line was now on the "fall," too, all the way to the Atlantic across the plains.

From this place there is a branch line to Denver City, the chief town of Colorado, which is rich in gold and silver mines, and possesses more than fifty thousand inhabitants.

Thirteen hundred and eighty-two miles had now been accomplished in three days and three nights. Four nights and four days would now be sufficient to reach New York, and Phileas Fogg had hitherto lost no time.

During the night Walbat Camp was left behind, Lodgepool Creek was also passed, and at eleven o'clock they entered Nebraska State, passing close to Sedgwick and Julesburg on the southern bank of the Platte River.

Here the Union Pacific Railroad was inaugurated by General Dodge on the 23rd of October, 1867; the trains full of guests were stopped; three cheers were given for the President. The Indians had a sham

153

fight, fireworks were displayed, and the first number of the *Railway Pioneer* newspaper was printed in the train. So this great line was inaugurated—the instrument of progress and civilization.

At eight o'clock in the morning Fort Macpherson was passed, and they were still three hundred and fifty-seven miles from Omaha. The railroad followed the windings of the Platte River, and at nine o'clock the train stopped at North Platte, which is built between the branches of the stream, which here unite. The 101st meridian had now been passed.

Mr. Fogg and his friends had resumed their whist, and did not complain of the length of the journey. Fix had begun by winning, but now seemed about to lose his money again, for all the morning fortune had favoured Mr. Fogg, the blushing honours came thick upon him, and trumps fell from his hands. At a moment when he was about to play a bold game and lead off with a spade, a voice behind said:

" If I were you I'd play a diamond."

The whist-players all looked round; Colonel Proctor was behind Mr. Fogg, and they recognized each other at once.

" Oh, it's you, is it?" said the colonel; " so you are going to play a spade, are you?"

" Yes, and I do play it," said Fogg as he threw down the ten.

" Well, then, I choose to have diamonds," replied Colonel Proctor insolently, and he made a gesture as if to pick up a card, adding: " You don't understand the game."

" Perhaps I shall be more skilful at another," replied Fogg, rising.

" You have only got to try, you son of a John Bull!" replied the stout man.

Mrs. Aouda was very pale; she seized Fogg by the

arm and pushed him gently back. Passepartout was ready to throw himself upon the American, who was gazing on Mr. Fogg in the most insulting manner. But Fix rose, and, approaching Proctor, said:

"You forget that this is my affair, sir; you have not only insulted me, but struck me."

"Mr. Fix," said Fogg, "I beg your pardon, but this concerns me alone. By pretending that I did wrong to play spades the colonel has insulted me, and he shall give me satisfaction."

"When you like, where you like, and with what weapons you like," replied the American.

Mrs. Aouda vainly tried to detain Mr. Fogg; the detective also endeavoured to make the quarrel his own; Passepartout wished to throw the colonel out of the window, but his master checked him by a sign. Mr. Fogg left the car, and the American followed him on to the platform.

"Sir," said Mr. Fogg to his adversary, "I am in a great hurry to return to Europe, and any delay will prejudice me greatly."

"What is that to me?" replied the colonel.

"Sir," continued Mr. Fogg politely, "after our encounter at San Francisco I made up my mind to return and find you out as soon as I had finished my business in Europe."

"Indeed!"

"Will you give me a meeting in six months?"

"Why not in six years?"

"I say six months," replied Mr. Fogg; "I will be punctual."

"That is nonsense," replied Proctor; "it must be now or not at all."

"Very well," replied Fogg; "are you going to New York?"

"No."

"To Chicago?"

" No."

" To Omaha?"

" That can't matter to you. Do you know Plum Creek?"

" No" replied Fogg.

" It is the next station. We shall be there in an hour and shall stop ten minutes; in that time we can arrange our little affair."

" Very well," replied Mr. Fogg, " I will stop at Plum Creek."

" And will stay there altogether," added the American insolently.

" Who knows?" replied Mr. Fogg as he entered the carriage again as coolly as ever.

He then essayed to cool Mrs. Aouda by assuring her that bullies were always cowards; he then secured Fix's services as second, and finally sat down to whist as if nothing had happened.

At eleven o'clock the whistle announced their approach to the station. Mr. Fogg rose, and, followed by Fix went out on the platform; Passepartout, carrying a brace of revolvers, accompanied them. Mrs. Aouda remained in the car as pale as death.

Just then the door of the opposite waggon opened, and Colonel Proctor appeared, followed by his second, a Yankee like himself; but just as the party were about to descend the guard ran up and stopped them, saying:

" You cannot get out, gentlemen."

" Why not?" asked the colonel.

" Because we are twenty minutes late, and we cannot stop."

" But I am going to fight with this gentleman."

" I am very sorry, gentlemen, but we must start at once; there is the gong sounding now." And as he spoke the train started.

" I am extremely sorry," said the conductor; "under other circumstances I should have been delighted to have obliged you; but there is nothing to prevent your fighting as you go along."

" Perhaps that would not suit the Britisher?" said Colonel Proctor with a sneer.

" It will suit me very well," replied Fogg.

" I can see that we are in America," thought Passepartout, " and the conductor is a gentleman of the highest breeding."

The two adversaries and their seconds, preceded by the conductor, passed down to the last car of the train, in which only a dozen people were seated. The conductor asked them to be good enough to go outside, as the two gentlemen were going to fight a duel. The passengers were only too pleased to oblige, and they went out.

The car, about fifty feet long, was very suitable for the purpose. The duellists could advance between the seats and fire at their ease. Nothing could be more simple. Mr. Fogg and Colonel Proctor, each carrying a brace of six-shooters, entered the car; the seconds locked them in, and returned to the platform. The first time the engine whistled they were to begin to fire, and after a lapse of two minutes their friends would carry out what remained of the two gentlemen.

Nothing could be more simple; in fact, it was so very simple that Fix and Passepartout could hear their hearts beat.

Everyone was on the alert for the first whistle, when suddenly savage cries were heard, and shots, which certainly did not come from the duellists, echoed through the train. The firing ran all along the cars. Cries of terror were heard from the interior.

Colonel Proctor and Mr. Fogg were immediately released, and rushed, revolvers in hand, in front of the train, when they perceived that it had been attacked by a band of Sioux Indians.

This was not the first time such a thing had occurred. The Indians leaped on the footboards as the train proceeded as easily as a circus-rider would upon a horse. Their first act was to get on the engine and to stun the engine-driver and fireman. One of them attempted to stop the train, but only succeeded in turning on the full pressure of the steam, and increasing the pace to a fearful extent.

Meantime others had climbed into the cars, and were now waging a hand-to-hand fight with the passengers; they threw the baggage from the waggons, and cries and detonations resounded in all directions.

However, the travellers defended themselves bravely; they barricaded the waggons, which now appeared like so many forts carried along at the rate of a hundred miles an hour.

Mrs. Aouda had behaved heroically, revolver in hand. She defended herself, and fired through the broken windows whenever she caught sight of a savage. About twenty of the assailants were shot or crushed by the wheels, and many of the passengers lay wounded on the seats.

The combat had already lasted ten minutes and if the train were not stopped the Sioux would be the victors. At Fort Kearney, two miles distant, there was a guard, and if that post were passed the Indians would be masters of the train before the next station was reached.

The conductor was fighting beside Mr. Fogg when he was shot. As he fell he exclaimed:

" We are all lost if the train be not stopped in less than five minutes."

" It shall be stopped," said Fogg as he attempted to pass out.

158

" Stay where you are, sir," said Passepartout. " This is my business."

Phileas Fogg had not time to stop his faithful follower, who managed to glide beneath the carriages unseen. With marvellous agility, and taking advantage of every cover, he managed to reach the front of the train in safety.

There, hanging with one hand between the baggage-waggon and the tender, with the other he managed to unfasten the coupling-chain. He would not have been able to have disconnected the drawbar if a fortunate jolt had not assisted him. The engine thus let loose sped away at a tremendous pace, while the train gradually slackened speed, and, with the assistance of the breaks, was stopped about a hundred paces from Kearney Station.

The soldiers were on the alert, and hastened to the assistance of the passengers, but the Indians did not await their coming. Before the train stopped the whole band had disappeared. But when the travellers assembled on the platform they found that several of their friends were missing, and, amongst others the brave Frenchman who had devoted himself to save them.

CHAPTER XXX

In which Phileas Fogg fairly does his duty

Three travellers, including Passepartout, were missing, but whether they had been killed or taken prisoners was not known.

Several had been wounded, but none mortally. Amongst those most grievously hurt was Colonel Proctor, who had fought bravely. He was carried into the station with the others, and his immediate wants attended to.

159

Mrs. Aouda was unhurt. Phileas Fogg had not received a scratch. Fix was slightly wounded in the arm, but Passepartout was missing, and the young lady could not repress her tears.

The travellers all left the carriages, the wheels of which were covered with blood and jagged pieces of flesh. Long crimson tracks were visible on the whitened surface of the plain, and the last files of the Sioux were disappearing in the south.

Mr. Fogg, with arms crossed, stood motionless. He had to make up his mind on a grave question. Mrs. Aouda looked at him without speaking, but they undertsood each other. If his servant had been taken prisoner, was it not his duty to rescue him from the Indians?

" I will bring him back, dead or alive," he said simply.

" Oh, Mr. Fogg!" exclaimed the young lady as she seized his hand and covered it with tears.

" And living," added Mr. Fogg, " if we make haste."

By this resolve Fogg sacrificed everything; he pronounced his own ruin. One day's delay would cause him to lose the New York steamer and his wager, but he considered it his duty to act as he was doing, and he did not hesitate.

The commandant of Fort Kearney was there; his company was under arms.

" Sir," said Mr. Fogg, " three of our fellow-passengers are missing."

" Dead?" asked the captain.

" Dead or prisoners," replied Fogg, " we must make sure. Is it your intention to pursue the Sioux?"

" That is a grave question," replied the captain. " The Indians may retreat beyond the Arkansas. I cannot abandon the fort."

" But," urged Fogg, " the lives of three men are in the balance."

160

"No doubt, but I cannot risk fifty lives to save three."

"I do not know whether you can or not, sir," replied Fogg, "but I know you ought."

"Sir!" replied the captain, "no one here can teach me my duty."

"Very well," said Phileas Fogg coldly, "then I will go alone."

"You!" exclaimed Fix, "going alone in pursuit of the Indians?"

"Do you expect me to let that unfortunate man perish, to whom everyone here owes his life? Of course I shall go."

"No, you shall not go alone," replied the captain, moved in spite of himself; "you are a brave man. I want thirty volunteers," he added, turning to his men.

The whole company stepped forward at once. The captain had only to choose. Thirty picked men were told off, and an old sergeant placed in command.

"Thank you, captain," said Mr. Fogg.

"May I not accompany you?" said Fix.

"You may if you please, but if you wish to do me a kindness you will remain with Mrs. Aouda, in case anything should happen to me."

Fix turned pale. Was he justified in separating himself from the man he had followed so persistently for so long? Ought he to leave him to wander about in the desert? The detective gazed steadily at Mr. Fogg, but notwithstanding his opinion of that gentleman, he could not sustain his calm frank look.

"I will remain," he said.

Mr. Fogg having shaken hands with Mrs. Aouda and confided his precious bag to her care, started with his escort.

But before he quitted the station he said to the soldiers, "My lads, I will give you a thousand pounds if we save the prisoners."

It was then a few minutes past twelve o'clock. Mrs. Aouda retired to the waiting-room, and remained thinking of Phileas Fogg, of his simple generosity and grand courage. He had sacrificed his fortune and was now risking his life, without the slightest hesitation, for what he considered his duty. In Mrs. Aouda's eyes Phileas Fogg was a hero.

But Fix did not think so; he could not conceal his agitation, and kept walking up and down the platform; but after some consideration he recovered himself. Now that Fogg had gone, the detective perceived how foolish he had been to let him go; he had actually consented to lose sight of the man whom he had followed round the world. He blamed himself and found fault with his own acts as if he had been an inspector of police reprimanding a constable.

"How foolish I have been!" he thought. "The other one has gone, and will not return; he has told who I am; but how is it that I have been made such a fool of, and with the warrant of arrest actually in my pocket?"

Thus the inspector reasoned as he walked up and down slowly. He did not know what to do. Sometimes he felt inclined to tell Mrs. Aouda everything, but he knew how she would receive the news. What was he to do? He was tempted at one time to go in pursuit of Fogg, and thought it would not be difficult to find him if he followed the tracks in the snow, but another fall would at once efface them.

Fix felt very much discouraged and equally inclined to give up the game. He had now an opportunity to go home if he wished, for about two o'clock in the afternoon, while the snow was again falling heavily, a long whistle of a locomotive was heard from the eastward. An enormous shadow enveloped in a fantastic light advanced slowly, appearing twice its usual size in consequence of the fog. This was the locomotive which was detached from the train, which had continued its journey with the driver and stoker lying senseless on the foot-plate. It had run for some miles beyond Fort Kearney, and then the steam having gone down for want of fuel it came to a standstill.

Neither the driver nor stoker was mortally wounded, and after a time they recovered consciousness.

They found themselves in the prairie without the train; they at length recollected what had happened. The driver had no doubt he would find his train somewhere on the line, and although it was dangerous to return, and would have been more prudent to have gone on to Omaha, he did not hesitate, but ran back whistling through the mist.

The passengers were all delighted to see the engine again, that they could resume their journey.

When the engine arrived Mrs. Aouda left the waiting-room and asked the guard when he was going to start.

" This moment, madame."

" But our poor friends the prisoners?"

" I mustn't stop the service," he replied; " we are already three hours behind time."

" When will the next train come from San Francisco?"

" To-morrow evening, madame."

" To-morrow evening! that will be too late. You must wait."

" It can't be done," replied the guard. " Get in, please, if you are going on."

" I shall not go," replied the young lady.

Fix heard this dialogue. A short time previously, before the engine had arrived, he had made up his mind to leave Kearney, but now there was nothing to prevent his going, he felt unable to go. The conflict

163

within him raged fiercer; his want of success aggravated him; he could fight to the end.

Meantime the travellers, including some of the wounded, amongst the latter Colonel Proctor, who was dangerously hurt, took their places in the train, which soon afterwards started. Fix remained behind.

The hours rolled slowly on; the weather was very bad and very cold. Fix remained seated motionless on a bench as if asleep. Mrs. Aouda, notwithstanding the storm, frequently walked to the end of the platform, and endeavoured to pierce the thickly-falling snow, but she could see nothing, and retired to her room only to come out again with the same result.

Night came on. The detachment had not returned. What could have happened to the soldiers? Had they lost their way, or had they been worsted in a fight? The captain was very anxious, though he tried not to betray his anxiety.

Night fell; the snow became less, but the cold increased; not a sound could be heard all night. Mrs. Aouda was very anxious, and imagined a thousand dangers. Fix remained almost motionless, but did not sleep nevertheless. At one time a man approached him and said something, but the detective merely shook his head in reply.

Thus the night passed. At sunrise objects could be seen at a distance of two miles; but towards the south, in which direction Fogg and his party were expected, nothing was visible.

Seven o'clock came and the captain did not know what to do. He was hesitating whether he should send a second detachment in search of the former, when a sound of firing was heard. The men rushed out of the fort, and at half-a-mile off they perceived the little troop returning in good order.

Mr. Fogg was marching in front, and close to them

were Passepartout and his two companions rescued from the Indians. They had encountered the Sioux about ten miles to the south of Kearney. Just before the arrival of the detachment the prisoners had turned upon their captors, three of whom the Frenchman had knocked down when his master and the soldiers arrived to succour him.

The whole party were welcomed with the greatest delight, and Fogg distributed the reward he had promised to the soldiers, and Passepartout confessed that he certainly cost his master very dear.

Fix looked at Mr. Fogg without speaking, and was unable to analyse his impressions just then. Mrs. Aouda, quite unable to speak, seized Mr. Fogg's hands, and pressed them in her own.

Passepartout, meanwhile, was looking for the train; he hoped to find it ready to start for Omaha, and trusted that the lost time might be made up.

" Where is the train?" he said.

" Gone," replied Fix.

" When does the next train arrive here?" asked Phileas Fogg.

" Not till evening."

" Ah!" replied the impassible gentleman.

CHAPTER XXXI

The detective forwards Mr. Fogg's interests very considerably

Phileas Fogg was now twenty hours behind time. Passepartout, the involuntary cause of the delay, was desperate. He had ruined his master.

The detective came up to Mr. Fogg, and said:

" Are you really in such a great hurry?"

" I am really," replied Mr. Fogg.

" I wish particularly to know. Must you be at New

York in time to catch the Liverpool steamer on the 11th?"

"I have a very great interest in doing so."

"And if your voyage had not been interrupted by the Indians you would have reached New York in time?"

"Yes, with twelve hours to spare."

"Well, you are now twenty hours late. You have eight hours to make up. Will you try to do so?"

"On foot?"

"No, in a sledge—a sledge with sails. A man here has suggested it to me."

This was the man who had spoken to Fix during the night, and whose offer the detective had refused.

Phileas Fogg did not reply, but when Fix indicated the individual Fogg went and spoke to him. The pair soon entered a hut near the station, and there they found a sort of sledge large enough to hold five or six people. A high mast, with wire rope, supported an immense sail, and a sort of rudder was used for steering.

It was, in fact, a sledge like a cutter yacht on runners. In winter time, when the trains are snowed up, these sledges are frequently used, and with their immense sails, if the wind be favourable, they go quite as quickly as, if not quicker than, the locomotive.

The bargain was soon made. The west wind was in their favour. As the snow was hard, the owner of the sledge hoped to reach Omaha in a few hours. From that town there were plenty of trains to New York. It was not impossible that they might regain the lost time. At all events they determined to try.

Mr. Fogg, unwilling to expose Aouda to the cold, suggested that she should remain with Passepartout and continue her journey more comfortably with him; but she declined, greatly to the delight of the valet, who did not wish to leave his master alone with Fix.

It was not easy to guess at the detective's thoughts. Whether his conviction concerning Fogg was shaken or not it was impossible to say, but he would do his duty in any case, and hasten Fogg's return to England as much as possible.

At eight o'clock the sledge was ready. The travellers took their places and wrapped themselves up, the two immense sails were hoisted, and impelled by the high wind they sped over the snow at forty miles an hour.

From Fort Kearney to Omaha is two hundred miles in a bee-line, as Americans say. If the wind held and no accident happened they would reach Omaha at one p.m.

It was a wonderful journey. The travellers were huddled together voiceless from cold; the sledge glided along like a boat on a lake. When the wind blew strongly they were almost lifted from the ground; the owner at the helm steered them straight, and though they had no means of ascertaining their exact speed, they could not be going less than forty miles an hour.

" If nothing breaks," said Mudge, the owner, " we shall arrive in time."

He had an interest in reaching his journey's end in time, for Fogg, as usual, had promised him a handsome premium.

The prairie was perfectly flat, and Mudge took the chord of the arc described by the railroad which follows the river. The steersman was not afraid of being stopped by the river, for it was frozen. There was nothing to fear but an accident or a change of wind, but the wind continued steady, and even increased. It hummed through the wire rigging as through harp-strings. The sledge rushed along with its plaintive accompaniment.

" The wires give the fifth and the octave," observed Mr. Fogg.

167

This was the only remark he made all the time. Mrs. Aouda, carefully wrapped up, was protected from the cold. Passepartout, his face as red as the sun in a mist, was now more confident of reaching New York in time for the steamer. He even felt inclined to shake Fix by the hand in acknowledgment of his having procured the sledge, but the same hope kept him quiet. In any case there was one thing Passepartout would never forget, and that was his rescue by Mr. Fogg, who had risked his life and fortune for him.

While the travellers indulged in thought the sledge still rushed along. Nothing but snow could be seen. The space between the Union Pacific Railway and the branch to St. Joseph appeared like a great uninhabited island. There was no house of any description to be seen. Occasionally a gaunt tree was passed, or a flock of birds arose around them, or a pack of wolves followed the sledge; but Passepartout, revolver in hand, was ready for them, though, if any accident had happened, the travellers would have run great risks. However, the sledge still sped on, and the howling brutes were left far behind.

At midday Mudge thought they were crossing the Platte River, and, although he said nothing, he was sure that Omaha was within twenty miles.

In fact, in less than an hour he hauled down the sails, and the sledge ran on for half a mile farther without them. At length it stopped, and Mudge, pointing to some snow-covered roofs, exclaimed:

"We have arrived!"

He was right. Passepartout and Fix jumped down and stretched their stiffened limbs. Then they assisted Mr. Fogg and Mrs. Aouda to alight. Phileas having rewarded Mudge handsomely, and Passepartout having shaken hands most warmly, the travellers rushed to the railway station.

The express was waiting, and they jumped in. They had seen nothing of the town, but they did not regret it.

The train started. During the night they crossed the Mississippi, and the next day, the 10th, at four p.m., they reached Chicago, already rebuilt, and rising more proudly than ever on the borders of the beautiful Michigan Lake.

They were still nine hundred miles from New York, but there was no want of trains, and they passed from one to another. Starting again at full speed, they crossed Indiana, Ohio, Pennsylvania, and New Jersey. The plain of the Hudson appeared at last, and on the 11th of December, at a quarter-past eleven at night, the train stopped at the station on the right bank of the river, before the pier from which the Cunard steamers start.

The *China* had left for Liverpool only five-and-forty minutes previously.

CHAPTER XXXII

Phileas Fogg struggles against his bad luck

The *China* had carried away Mr. Fogg's last hope. No other steamer would be of the slightest use, none of the White Star, nor Transatlantic, nor the Inman, nor the Hamburg American could assist him, for if he had taken his passage on any of them he must have been too late to win his wager. Mr. Fogg learnt all these particulars from *Bradshaw's Guide*.

Passepartout was half-mad at losing the steamer by three-quarters of an hour. It was all his fault; and when he looked back over the incidents of the journey, the sums of money expended for him, the amount of the wager involved, and all the expenses of the trip now rendered useless, he could have killed himself.

169

But Mr. Fogg did not reproach him. As he left the landing-stage he only said: " Come along; we will see what we can do to-morrow."

They drove to the *Saint Nicholas Hotel* in the Broadway for the night, but only Mr. Fogg was able to sleep.

The next day was the 12th of December, and there were now only nine days thirteen hours and forty-five minutes left. If Mr. Fogg had left in the *China* he would have won his wager.

He left the hotel alone, and telling the others to be ready for a sudden start, he went to the Hudson River to look for a ship. There were plenty of vessels getting ready for sea, but no steamers apparently. At last Mr. Fogg noticed a small screw vessel, which had all the appearance of being about to start immediately. Hailing a boat, Mr. Fogg was soon on board the *Henrietta*, which was an iron steamer, and asked to see the captain.

A man of about fifty, a regular sea-wolf, approached.

" Are you the captain?" asked Mr. Fogg.

" I am."

" I am Phileas Fogg from London."

" I am Andrew Speedy from Cardiff."

" You will soon start?"

" In an hour."

" Whither bound?"

" Bordeaux."

" What cargo do you carry?"

" None. I am in ballast."

" Have you any passengers?"

" I never carry passengers; they are always in the way."

" Does your ship steam rapidly?"

" Between eleven and twelve knots."

" Will you take me and three others to Liverpool?"

" To Liverpool?   Why not to China?"

" I said to Liverpool."

" No."

" No?"

" No.   I say I am bound to Bordeaux, and to Bordeaux I go."

" Is money any object?"

" Not the least."

The captain's tone admitted of no reply.

" But the owners of the *Henrietta*——" suggested Fogg.

" I am the owner; the ship belongs to me."

" I will hire her."

" No you won't."

" I'll buy her, then."

" No.   She is not for sale."

Mr. Fogg did not show the slightest disappointment though the situation was grave.   Things were not as they had been at Hong Kong, and the captain of the *Henrietta* was not like the owner of the *Tankadère*. Hitherto money had had effect; now, apparently, it was of no use.

However, it was necessary to cross the Atlantic somehow or another, by boat or balloon, and Phileas Fogg had made up his mind, for he said to the captain:

" Well, won't you take me to Bordeaux?"

" No, not if you were to give me two hundred dollars."

" I will give you two thousand."

" For each one?"

" Yes."

" And there are four of you?"

" Yes."

At this Captain Speedy scratched his head.   Eight thousand dollars to be made without going out of his way!   This was enough to remove his antipathy to all passengers. Besides, passengers at such a rate became precious merchandise.

"I start at nine o'clock," said Captain Speedy shortly, "and if you are here then, why, here you are."

"At nine o'clock we shall be here," replied Fogg.

It was then half-past eight. It did not take Mr. Fogg very long to drive up to the hotel and to return with Mrs. Aouda, Passepartout, and even the inseparable Fix, to whom Mr. Fogg offered a passage, which the detective accepted with his usual coolness. They were all on board by the time the *Henrietta* cast off.

When Passepartout learnt what this last passage was likely to cost, he uttered a series of oaths which descended through all the scales.

As for Fix, he made up his mind that the Bank of England would not recover much of its money, for he calculated, even if Mr. Fogg did not spend any more, that at least seven thousand pounds had been disbursed.

CHAPTER XXXIII

Phileas Fogg rises to the occasion

An hour after this the *Henrietta* passed the lightship at the entrance of the Hudson, rounded Sandy Hook, and sped out to sea. During the day Long Island and Fire Island were passed, and then the course was laid eastward.

Next day, the 13th December, at noon, Mr. Fogg ascended to the bridge, for Captain Speedy was locked up in his cabin, where he was using very strong language, which, under the circumstances, was almost justifiable.

The facts were very simple. Mr. Fogg wished to go to Liverpool, and Captain Speedy did not, so the former having accepted the passage to Bordeaux, made such good use of his money amongst the sailors and the engineers, who were not on good terms with the captain, that he had gained them to his own side, and so Phileas Fogg actually commanded the ship in lieu of Captain Speedy, who was shut up in the cabin, and the ship was heading for Liverpool. It was evident by the way Mr. Fogg managed the vessel that he knew something of seamanship.

Later on we shall see how the adventure terminated. Meantime Mrs. Aouda was very anxious, but said nothing. Fix was quite upset, but Passepartout looked upon it as a good joke.

The captain had told Mr. Fogg that the *Henrietta* would steam between eleven and twelve knots an hour, and he was right.

If—for there were still " ifs "—if the sea did not get up, if the wind did not shift, and if nothing happened to the machinery, it was not impossible that the *Henrietta* would reach Liverpool within the specified time; but then awkward questions would probably arise about the *Henrietta*, as well as respecting the Bank affair.

All went well at first, and the *Henrietta*, under sail and steam, behaved like an Atlantic liner.

Passepartout was delighted. This last exploit of his master pleased him most of all. The crew had never seen such a cheerful active fellow as he became ; he made friends all round, and they worked like heroes for him. His good-humour was infectious: all past troubles and perils were forgotten; nothing was thought of but the successful attainment of their object, and meantime the worthy fellow kept his eye upon Fix, but their former intimacy no longer existed.

Indeed, Fix did not understand what was going on ; he was perfectly astonished at the capture of the *Henrietta*, the bribery of the crew, and at Mr. Fogg having taken the command. The detective knew not what to think, for, after all, a gentleman who had begun by stealing fifty thousand pounds might end by stealing a vessel, and Fix not unnaturally decided in his own mind that Fogg would not go to Liverpool at all, but would seek some other port where he could turn pirate and live in safety. On the whole, the detective rather regretted having been mixed up in the affair.

Captain Speedy meanwhile continued to swear in his cabin, and Passepartout, who took him his meals, was obliged to be very careful; but Fogg took no notice whatever of him.

On the 13th they passed the banks of Newfoundland. This is a very dangerous locality, where fogs are frequent and gales are violent. The barometer had been falling all the day before, and consequently during the night they found the temperature lower and the wind rising in the south-east.

This was unlucky, but Mr. Fogg would not go out of his way, so he furled the sails and put on full pressure. Nevertheless, the speed became less, and the vessel pitched tremendously in the long sea. The wind rose more and more, and it seemed as if the *Henrietta* would not be able to hold on her course. If she had to scud all hope of winning the wager would be lost.

Passepartout's countenance was as dark as the heavens, but Phileas Fogg was a bold sailor, and kept the ship's head to sea without even banking up the fires. The *Henrietta* now cut through the waves, and was swept fore and aft; the screw was frequently high out of the water, but still progress was made.

All this time the wind, though it did not rise to a hurricane, continued very strong from the south-east, and no sail could be hoisted, and thus a great assistance to the screw was lost.

On the 16th of December—the seventy-fifth day from London—half the voyage across the ocean had been accomplished and the worst of it was over. Had it been in the summer success would have been certain, but in the winter it was different. Passepartout said nothing; he trusted in the steam even if the wind failed them.

But on the same day the engineer came to Mr. Fogg and spoke to him with an anxious countenance. Without knowing why, Passepartout felt uneasy. He would have given one of his ears to have heard what passed, but he only caught an observation of Mr. Fogg's.

"You are quite certain of what you say?"

"Quite certain, sir," replied the engineer. "You must not forget that we have been running at full speed since we started, and although we had enough coal to carry us to Bordeaux at half-pressure, we had not enough to go at full speed to Liverpool."

"I will think of what you say," replied Mr. Fogg.

Passepartout now understood it all. The coal was failing. "If my master can conquer this," he thought, "he is a clever fellow."

He could not help confiding in Fix, who said:

"So you still think we are going to Liverpool?"

"Of course."

"Idiot!" replied the detective, who shrugged his shoulders and walked away.

Passepartout was on the point of compelling an explanation when he reflected that the unfortunate Fix was probably greatly disappointed and humiliated at having so foolishly followed a false scent round the world, so he did nothing.

Now what would Mr. Fogg do now? It was impossible to say, but it appeared that he had made up his mind, for he told the engineer to keep up at full speed as long as possible.

The result was that on the 18th the engineer came up and told him that the coal was almost exhausted.

" Keep up the pressure as long as you can," replied Mr. Fogg.

About noon the same day, after taking the reckoning, Mr. Fogg told Passepartout to release Captain Speedy. The valet would as soon have unchained a tiger, but he went as he was bidden, muttering, " How savage he will be!"

Shortly afterwards a bombshell came on deck. This bomb was Captain Speedy, and he looked ready to burst.

" Where are we?" he roared as soon as his anger permitted him speech; " where are we?"

" Seven hundred and seventy miles from Liverpool," replied Mr. Fogg calmly.

" You pirate!" roared Speedy.

" I have sent for you, sir——"

" Robber!"

" To ask you to sell me your ship," continued Fogg.

" No, by all the devils—no!"

" Then I must burn her."

" Burn my ship?"

" Yes, the upper works at any rate; we want fuel."

" Burn my ship!" spluttered Speedy, who was so angry he could hardly speak; " why she's worth fifty thousand dollars!"

" Here are sixty thousand dollars," replied Phileas Fogg, offering him a roll of bank-notes.

This had a tremendous effect upon Andrew Speedy; the bank-notes were too much for him. In an instant he forgot his anger, his imprisonment, and complaints against his passengers. The ship was twenty years old. His fortune was made. The bomb had not burst; Mr. Fogg had pulled out the fuse.

"I suppose I may still keep the hulk?" Speedy said in a milder tone.

"Yes, that and the machinery are yours. Is it a bargain?"

"It is," replied Speedy as he put the notes in his pocket.

While this arrangement was being concluded Passepartout was as white as a sheet, while Fix looked as if he was going to have a fit. Nearly twenty thousand pounds were expended, and Fogg had relinquished the most valuable portions of the vessel. It was true that fifty-five thousand pounds had been stolen from the Bank.

When Andrew Speedy had put the money in his pocket, Mr. Fogg said:

"You must know that if I do not reach London by the 21st I shall lose twenty thousand pounds, so you need not be astonished. I lost the steamer at New York, and as you refused to take me to Liverpool——"

"And I was right," said the captain, "for I have made twenty thousand dollars. But do you know one thing, you are a bit of a Yankee, Captain Fogg."

Having paid his passenger this compliment, as he fancied, he was going down, when Fogg said:

"Now the ship is mine?"

"Certainly, from keel to truck—that is, the woodwork, of course."

"Quite so. Will you have the interior fittings cut away for fuel, please?"

This course was absolutely necessary, and that day the poop, the cabin-fittings, and the spar-deck were cut up.

Next day, the 19th December, the spars and masts were burnt, the whole crew assisting in the demolition. The following day the bulwarks, etc., were cut away, and the *Henrietta* was now a mere hulk. But that afternoon they sighted the Fastnet light on the Irish coast. At ten p.m. they passed Queenstown. Phileas Fogg had only twenty-four hours to reach London, even if he could have kept up full speed to Liverpool; but the steam was giving out.

"Sir," said Captain Speedy, who was now much interested, "everything is against you, and we are only now passing Queenstown."

"Is that Queenstown where we see the lights?"

"Yes."

"Can we enter?"

"Not before three o'clock, at high water."

"We must wait," replied Fogg quietly, without moving a muscle of his countenance, nor indicating that he was about to make a last effort for success.

Queenstown is the port where the transatlantic steamers land the American mails, which are then forwarded by express trains and steamers *viâ* Dublin and Holyhead to London, and twelve hours are gained upon the quickest steamers to Liverpool. Mr. Fogg hoped to gain this time, and if he could reach Liverpool at noon next day he could get to London at a quarter to nine at night.

About one in the morning the *Henrietta* entered the harbour, and Mr. Fogg, wringing Captain Speedy's hand, went ashore with his friends. Fix was very much inclined to arrest Mr. Fogg on the spot, but he did not do so; but why he refrained he scarcely knew. At any rate he would not abandon him. The whole party got into a train at half-past one a.m., reached Dublin at daybreak, and soon afterwards embarked in one of the mail steamers, which, disdaining to rise upon the sea, cuts through it.

At twenty minutes to twelve a.m. Phileas Fogg landed at Liverpool.[1] He was then only six hours' distance from London.

[1] Query, Holyhead.—*Trans.*

At that moment Fix approached him, warrant in hand, and touching him on the shoulder said:

" Are you really Mr. Phileas Fogg?"

" Yes."

" Then I arrest you in the Queen's name."

CHAPTER XXXIV

Passepartout makes use of some very strong terms

Phileas Fogg was arrested. He was shut up in the Custom House pending his removal to London.

If Passepartout had not been seized by some policemen he would have attacked Fix when he arrested his master. Mrs. Aouda, quite overcome, could not understand the case, and when Passepartout explained the circumstances to her she wept bitterly.

Fix, rightly or wrongly, had only done his duty, and a jury would have to decide whether Fogg was guilty or not.

But then Passepartout recollected that all this trouble was owing to him. If he had only told Mr. Fogg all he knew concerning Fix, the latter would not have travelled at his master's expense, and Mr. Fogg would not have been arrested. He could so easily have proved his innocence on the journey. When he thought of this, Passepartout could have shot himself in his compunction.

Neither Mrs. Aouda nor the valet left the Custom House steps, notwithstanding the coldness of the weather. They wanted to see Mr. Fogg again.

As for that gentleman, he was completely ruined. The arrest had cost him his fortune. He had nearly eight hours and forty-five minutes to reach the Reform Club, and he could have got to London in six. But at that moment he was calmly sitting on a wooden bench, outwardly as unmoved as possible, not withstanding the rage boiling within him. Did he still hope?

He had carefully placed his watch before him on the table, and was following the movement of the hands. Not a word escaped him, but his expression was fixed.

Whether honest or not, his situation was a most unfortunate one. If honest, he was a ruined man; if dishonest, he was a convict.

Was he still thinking of success or escape? Perhaps so, for he frequently got up and walked round the room, but doors and windows were all closed and barred.

At length he sat down, and, taking his note-book from his pocket, he read the following:

" Twenty-first December, Saturday. Liverpool."

To this he added:

" Eightieth day, 11.40 a.m."

The clock struck one. Mr. Fogg noticed that his watch was two minutes fast.

The clock struck two. If even now he could get into the express train he would reach London in time.

At thirty-three minutes past two a noise of the doors opening was heard, and he could distinguish the voices of Passepartout and Fix. Mr. Fogg's eyes glistened, the door was flung suddenly open, and Mrs. Aouda, Passepartout, and Fix rushed in.

The detective was out of breath.

" Sir," he gasped, " I beg your pardon—a most unfortunate resemblance. The real culprit has been arrested. You are free."

Phileas Fogg was free, and the first use he made of his recovered liberty was to advance upon the detective, and with a single blow he knocked him down.

" Well hit!" exclaimed Passepartout.

180

Fix lay on the ground without speaking. He had got what he deserved. The three travellers immediately jumped into a cab and drove to the railway station.

Mr. Fogg asked when there was a train for London. It was then two-forty p.m. The express had left five-and-thirty minutes previously.

Mr. Fogg ordered a special.

There were plenty of engines in steam, but the train could not be got ready before three o'clock.

At that hour Phileas Fogg, having given a hint to the engine-driver respecting a " tip," was rushing up to London, accompanied by Mrs. Aouda and his faithful servant.

The distance between London and Liverpool was accomplished in five hours and a half, a very easy thing when the line is quite clear. But there were some unavoidable checks, and when the train reached London it was ten minutes to nine.

Phileas Fogg, having gone round the world, had reached home five minutes too late.

He had lost his bet.

CHAPTER XXXV

Passepartout does not need bidding twice

Next day the inhabitants of Savile Row would scarcely have believed that Mr. Fogg had returned had they been told so, for the house was still closely shut up.

When he left the railway station he told Passepartout to buy some provisions and had then gone home.

He still retained his habitual impassibility, although he had been ruined by the detective's blunders. After his long journey, after having overcome a thousand obstacles and braved a thousand dangers, and even found time to do good *en route*, to fail at the very moment of success was terrible. Of the large sum he

181

had taken with him but a very small portion remained. His whole fortune, twenty thousand pounds, was deposited at Barings', and he owed this to the colleagues of the club. Having paid all expenses he would have been no richer had he won his bet, nor did he wish to be richer. He only bet for reputation. This wager ruined him altogether, but he had made up his mind what to do.

A room in the house had been reserved for Mrs. Aouda. She was in great distress, for she fancied Mr. Fogg meditated some serious act. Passepartout was afraid his master would commit suicide as eccentric Englishmen occasionally do, so he kept watch on him.

His first act, however, was to extinguish the gas which had been burning for eighty days. In the letter-box he had found the Company's bill, and he thought it was high time to put a stop to that expense.

Night passed, but it may be questioned whether Mr. Fogg got any rest. Certainly neither Mrs. Aouda nor Passepartout slept, for the latter kept watch at his master's door.

Next day Mr. Fogg told him to attend to Mrs. Aouda. He excused himself from joining her at meals as he wished to put his affairs in order; but that evening he asked for a few minutes' interview with her.

Passepartout, though he had received his orders, was unable to leave his master's room; his heart was full; he was torn by remorse, and blamed himself more than ever for the irreparable disaster. Only if he had but warned Mr. Fogg of Fix's intentions, his master would certainly have never brought the detective to Liverpool, and then——

Passepartout could contain himself no longer.

"Oh, sir, oh, Mr. Fogg," he cried, "do you not curse me? It is my fault that——"

"I blame no one," replied Phileas Fogg in his calmest tone. "Go."

Passepartout left the room and told Mrs. Aouda what his instructions were.

"Madame," he added, "I can do nothing. I have no influence with my master. Perhaps you——"

"What influence do I possess?" replied the lady. "Mr. Fogg will never give way to anyone. Does he understand how grateful I am? But he must not be left alone. You say that he wishes to see me this evening?"

"Yes, madame—no doubt to make arrangements for your stay in England."

"Let us wait," replied Mrs. Aouda thoughtfully.

So all that Sunday the house in Savile Row appeared uninhabited, and for the first time in his life Phileas Fogg did not go to his club at half-past eleven.

Why should he go? His friends did not expect him; as he had not made his appearance there to win the wager, his bet was lost. It was not even necessary for him to go to the Bank to draw his money; his adversaries had the cheque, and they had only to fill it up and present it.

Mr. Fogg, then, having nothing to go out for, remained at home and put his affairs in order. Passepartout kept running up and down stairs, and the time passed very slowly; he listened at his master's door without thinking it wrong; he even looked through the keyhole, for he feared something might happen. Sometimes he thought of Fix, but not unkindly; he wished him no wrong; he had been mistaken, like everyone else, about Phileas Fogg, and the detective had only done his duty, while he himself—— This thought haunted him and made him very miserable.

At last he could remain alone no longer, so he

tapped at the door of Mrs. Aouda's sitting-room, and being told to enter, sat down in the corner and looked at the young lady without speaking. She was also very pensive.

At about half-past seven Mr. Fogg came to know if Mrs. Aouda would speak with him, and Passepartout left the room.

Mr. Fogg took a chair opposite to her; he appeared as calm and impassible as ever.

For a few moments he made no remark; then, looking at Mrs. Aouda, he said:

"Madame, can you forgive me for having brought you to England?"

"I, Mr. Fogg?" she exclaimed as she endeavoured to check the beating of her heart.

"Permit me to finish," he continued. "When I took you away from India, which was dangerous for you, I was rich, and I hoped to be able to place a portion of my fortune at your disposal. You would then have been free and happy. Now I am ruined."

"I know it, Mr. Fogg," she replied, "and I have to seek your pardon for having followed you, and perhaps by retarding you have contributed to your losses."

"Madame, you could not have remained in India, and taking you away from those fanatics was the only thing to do."

"And, Mr. Fogg, you were not content to snatch me from a horrible death, but you also wished to insure my happiness in this country."

"Yes, madame," replied Fogg, "but circumstances were adverse; but the little I have left I wish to place at your disposal."

"But what will become of you?" she asked.

"Of me?" he repeated coldly. "I want for nothing."

" But how will you bear what is in store for you?"

" I will do my best," replied Mr. Fogg.

" In any case your friends will not permit you to want anything."

" I have no friends, madame."

" Your relations——"

" I have no relatives."

" Oh, then, I do indeed pity you, Mr. Fogg. Isolation is a very sad thing. Is there no one to whom you can confide your grief? For grief shared is more easily borne."

" So they say," replied Mr. Fogg.

" Mr. Fogg," said Mrs. Aouda, rising and extending her hand, " do you wish to possess at once a relative and a friend? Will you accept me for your wife?"

Mr. Fogg rose hastily; there was an unusual light in his eyes, and his lips were trembling. Mrs. Aouda looked at him steadily; the sincerity, the firmness, and sweetness of her glance penetrated him. For a moment he closed his eyes as if to avoid her gaze, and when he opened them again he said simply:

" I love you. In truth, by all I hold sacred, I love you, and am yours for ever!"

" Ah!" exclaimed Mrs. Aouda as he pressed her hand to his heart.

The bell was immediately rung for Passepartout. He came up at once. Mr. Fogg was holding the lady's hand. Passepartout understood the circumstances in a moment, and his face brightened considerably.

Mr. Fogg asked him whether it were too late to notify the intended marriage to the Rector of Marylebone.

Passepartout smiled, and replied it was never too late.

It was then five minutes past eight.

" It will be for to-morrow?" asked Passepartout.

" We may say to-morrow (Monday)?" said Mr. Fogg to Mrs. Aouda.

"To-morrow," she murmured; and Passepartout hurried away as fast as his legs would carry him.

CHAPTER XXXVI

Phileas Fogg is again at a premium in the market

It is time we said something of the change in public opinion when the real Bank robber, one James Strand, was arrested in Edinburgh on the 17th of December.

Three days before Phileas Fogg had been looked upon as a robber; now he was merely an eccentric person journeying round the world.

There was a great discussion in the papers. All those who had laid wagers on his success or failure rose up again as if by magic. The bonds became saleable, and took an upward tendency, until the name of Phileas Fogg was at a premium on the Exchange.

The five members of the Reform Club were not very comfortable during those three days. Would he return? Where was he on that 17th of December, the 76th day on his journey? Had he renounced the struggle, or was he still proceeding slowly? And, more than all, would he appear as agreed, at a quarter to nine p.m. on Saturday, the 21st of December?

During those three days society was intensely agitated. Telegrams were sent to America and Asia to obtain news of Mr. Fogg, and messengers were frequently dispatched to Savile Row without success. The police even could not tell what had become of Fix, and all this time the betting went on, and bonds were quoted no longer at a hundred per cent. discount, but at five and ten, and old Lord Albemarle actually got in at par.

So on that Saturday evening a great crowd had assembled in Pall Mall and the neighbourhood. The traffic was interfered with, and the crowd made bets, disputed, and argued all the time. The police had much difficulty to restrain the crowd, and as the hour approached the excitement rose at a tremendous pitch.

Mr. Fogg's five friends met at eight o'clock in the drawing-room of the club. John Sullivan, Samuel Fallentin, Andrew Stuart, Gautier Ralph, and Thomas Flanagan all awaited with anxiety the appearance of Mr. Fogg.

At twenty-five minutes past eight Stuart rose from his seat and said, "In twenty minutes, gentlemen, the time will have expired."

"When is the train from Liverpool due?" asked Thomas Flanagan.

"At seven twenty-three," replied Ralph, "and no one other then till ten minutes past twelve."

"Well, gentlemen," continued Stuart, "if Fogg had come by the seven twenty-three train he would have been here by now. We may look upon the bet as won, I think."

"We had better wait," replied Samuel Fallentin; "you know that our friend is very eccentric and is punctuality itself; he will not arrive too soon or too late, and I for one shall expect to see him at the last minute."

"If I were to see him I should not believe it was he," replied Andrew Stuart, who was very nervous.

"In fact," said Flanagan, "Mr. Fogg's project was ridiculous; whatever his own punctuality he could not prevent other people's delays, and two or three days' delay would throw him out altogether."

"Besides," added Sullivan, "we have had no news from him, though there are telegraphs all along the route."

"He has lost, gentlemen," continued Stuart, "a hundred times over. You know that the *China*, the only ship he could possibly have come over in to be in time, arrived yesterday, and Mr. Fogg's name does not appear in the passenger-list. On the most favourable computation our friend could scarcely have reached America, and I do not expect him for at least twenty days, so Lord Albemarle will be let in for his five thousand pounds."

"Then all we have to do," said Ralph, "is to present his cheque at Barings' to-morrow."

The clock was then pointing to twenty minutes to nine.

"Five minutes more," said Stuart.

The five friends looked at each other; their hearts, no doubt, were beating a little more quickly than usual, for the stakes were high even for such seasoned players. But they did not wish to show any anxiety, and at Fallentin's suggestion they sat down to the whist-table.

"I would not sell my share of the four thousand even if anyone were to offer me three thousand nine hundred and ninety-nine pounds."

The clock pointed to eighteen minutes to nine.

The players took their cards, but glanced at the clock every second. Though they felt quite secure, the minutes had never been so long in passing.

"Forty-three minutes past eight," said Flanagan, as he cut the cards handed him by Gautier Ralph.

There was a moment of perfect silence, and the roar of the crowd outside could be heard. The pendulum beat out the seconds, and the players counted every tick of the clock.

"Forty-four minutes past eight," said John Sullivan. His voice quivered a little with anxiety, which he could not repress.

In another minute they will have won their bet. They could no longer pretend to play—they counted every second.

At the fortieth second, and the fiftieth no news.

At the fifty-fifth a loud roar was heard outside, mingled with cheers and imprecations.

The five friends rose quickly.

At the fifty-seventh second the door of the drawing-room was opened, and before the pendulum had beat out the minute Phileas Fogg appeared, followed by an excited concourse of people who had forced their way into the club, and said in his usual calm voice:

" Here I am, gentlemen."

CHAPTER XXXVII

Showing how Phileas Fogg gained happiness by going round the world

Yes, it was Phileas Fogg himself!

It will be remembered that at five minutes past eight, about twenty-three hours after the travellers returned to London, Passepartout had been sent to arrange with the Rev. Samuel Wilson about the marriage of his master and Mrs. Aouda on the following morning.

Passepartout had hurried away, but the clergyman was not at home when he arrived at the house, and he had to wait about twenty minutes.

It was just twenty-five minutes past eight when he quitted the clergyman's house in a most disordered state and without his hat. He ran as fast as ever he could through the streets, overturning the passengers as he went.

In three minutes he was in Savile Row, and burst into Mr. Fogg's room quite breathless.

" What's the matter?" asked Mr. Fogg.

" The marriage is—impossible."

" Impossible?"

" Impossible for to-morrow."

" Why?"

" Because to-morrow is Sunday."

" Monday you mean," replied Mr. Fogg.

" No; to-day is Saturday."

" Saturday! Impossible!"

" It is! it is!" cried Passepartout. " You have made the mistake of a day. We arrived twenty-four hours in advance, but we have ten minutes left now."

Passepartout seized his master by the collar and dragged him to the door.

Phileas Fogg had no time to reflect. He rushed out of the house, jumped into a cab, promised the driver a hundred pounds, and so, having run over two dogs, and come into collision with five cabs, he arrived at the Reform Club at eight-forty-five exactly.

Thus Phileas Fogg had accomplished his tour of the world in eighty days, and had won his bet.

But how did it happen that such a very methodical man could have made the mistake of a day? How could he have thought that he had arrived on the evening of Saturday, the 21st of December, when it was actually Friday, the 20th, seventy-nine days after his departure?

The explanation is easy.

Phileas Fogg had gained a day without knowing it, as he travelled continually towards the east. Had he journeyed westward he would have lost a day.

For by travelling eastward he had gone southward, and consequently the days had diminished for him as many times four minutes as he passed degrees in that direction. There are 360 degrees in the earth's circumference, and these, multiplied by four minutes, give exactly twenty-four hours—in other words, Phileas Fogg had seen the sun rise eighty times while his friends in London had only seen it rise seventy-nine times. So that is how it happened that it was

Saturday, and not Sunday, as Mr. Fogg thought, and his friends awaited him at the Reform Club.

Passepartout's famous watch would have established this fact if it had marked the days as well as the hours.

Thus Phileas Fogg gained his twenty thousand pounds; but, as he had spent nearly nineteen thousand pounds, he did not win much. But he had not bet for money, and he divided the thousand pounds that remained between Passepartout and the unfortunate Fix, against whom he bore no malice, though he deducted the price of the gas that had been burning for one thousand nine hundred and twenty hours from Passepartout's share.

That same evening Mr. Fogg said to Aouda:

" Is our marriage still agreeable to you, madame?"

" I ought to ask you that question," she replied. " You are now rich."

" Excuse me, madame, that fortune is yours. If you had not thought of our marriage my servant would never have gone to Mr. Wilson, and I should not have found out my mistake. So——"

" Dear Mr. Fogg!" interrupted the young lady.

" My dearest Aouda," replied Mr. Fogg.

So all was settled, and forty-eight hours afterwards the marriage took place. Passepartout, beaming and blushing with happiness, gave away the bride. He had saved her life, and was entitled to that honour.

But early on the wedding morning Passepartout knocked loudly at his master's door.

Mr. Fogg opened it, and asked what was the matter.

" Why, sir, I have just discovered——"

" What?"

" That we could have gone round the world in seventy-eight days."

" No doubt," replied Mr. Fogg. " But if we had

not crossed India I should never have rescued Mrs. Aouda, you see."

And Mr. Fogg shut the door quietly.

Thus Phileas Fogg won his bet. He had gone round the world in eighty days, and had used every means of transport, steamers, railways, carriages, a yacht, a trading vessel, a sledge, and an elephant. The eccentric gentleman had displayed his marvellous qualities of punctuality and coolness. But, after all, what had he gained? How was he the better?

By nothing, you will say. Nothing! Very well, if a charming woman is nothing, who, extraordinary as it may appear, made him the happiest of men.

And now, reader, would you not go round the world for less?